Children's Big Book of
QUESTIONS
AND
ANSWERS

Sandy Creek
NEW YORK

Sandy Creek
NEW YORK

An Imprint of Sterling Publishing
387 Park Avenue South
New York, NY 10016

ISBN 978-1-4351-3677-9

Manufactured in GuangDong, China
Lot:
10 9 8 7 6 5 4 3
06/12

Children's Big Book of
QUESTIONS
AND
ANSWERS

Sandy Creek
NEW YORK

Contents

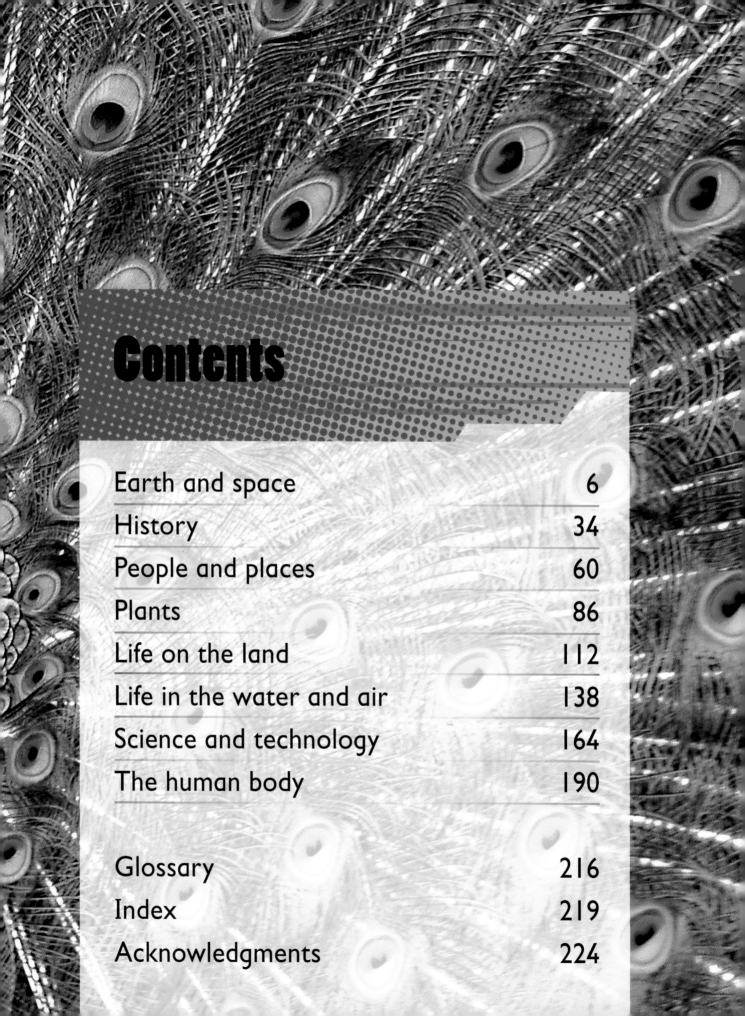

EARTH
AND SPACE

THE BIG BANG

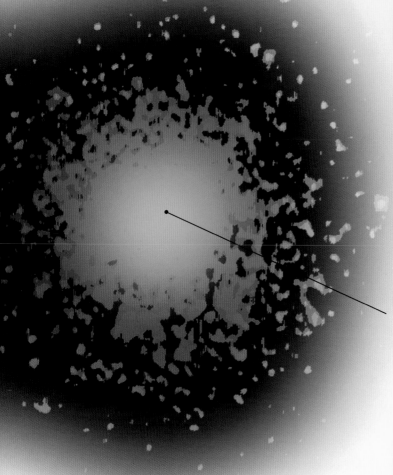

What was the Big Bang?

The Big Bang was an explosion that created the whole universe. About 14 billion years ago, the universe exploded outward from a hot, dense bubble that was smaller than a pinhead. The universe quickly grew larger than a galaxy and kept on expanding. As it slowly cooled, tiny particles (pieces) within it joined and began to form the stars and planets.

The Big Bang exploded from a tiny point called a singularity.

BELOW Stars begin as clouds of gas like this, called nebulae.

When did the first stars shine?

The first stars began to shine about 300 million years after the Big Bang. Particles began to clump together and formed clouds of gas. These slowly grew and became hotter and hotter. Eventually, the center of these clouds became so hot that the clouds exploded and became the balls of fire we call stars. New stars are born and die every day.

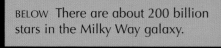
BELOW There are about 200 billion stars in the Milky Way galaxy.

HOW many galaxies are there?

There are more than 100 billion galaxies in the universe. A galaxy is a large group of stars, dust, gas, rocks, and planets. Most stars in the universe are found in galaxies. The Sun and planet Earth are part of our galaxy, the Milky Way. Astronomers have photographed many galaxies through special telescopes. With the naked eye, people can only see three galaxies beyond the Milky Way.

DID YOU KNOW?
Some of the stars we can see in the night sky are so far away that the light coming from them has taken millions of years to reach Earth.

IS the universe changing?

Yes, the universe is still growing and expanding today. Some scientists believe that the universe will keep expanding. Others think that the expansion will start to slow and eventually stop. They believe that the universe will then start to shrink until it crunches together into a tiny space and sparks off another Big Bang.

A telescope uses glass lenses to magnify distant objects.

THE SUN

What is the Sun?

The Sun is just an ordinary star, one of billions of stars in the universe. The Sun has a special name and is important to us because it is close enough to give Earth light and warmth. This light and warmth is what allows plants, animals, and other living things to survive on our planet. Without the Sun there would be no life on Earth.

BELOW Solar panels like these trap some of the Sun's energy and change it into electricity we can use. The word solar means "having to do with the Sun."

Close-up pictures of the Sun show the hot gases gushing out from its surface.

How hot is the Sun?

The temperature at the core, or center, of the Sun is about 29 million degrees Fahrenheit. From the core, this incredible heat energy flows to the surface, where the temperature is closer to 11,000 degrees Fahrenheit. This is still so incredibly hot that it would melt anything it touched.

Why is the Sun so bright?

The Sun is the brightest object in the sky because it is a giant ball of brightly glowing gas. Light from the Sun takes just over eight minutes to reach Earth, but when it gets here it is still so powerful that its light can damage your eyesight. That is why you should never look at the Sun directly and always wear sunglasses on sunny days.

DID YOU KNOW?
The Sun is about five billion years old and it is more than 600,000 miles wide. It is so big that more than one million Earths could fit inside it.

Solar eclipse seen here

MOON

EARTH

SUN

ABOVE The Sun is about 400 times wider than the Moon. However, because the Moon is about 400 times closer to Earth than the Sun, both the Moon and the Sun look about the same size in the sky from Earth.

When do solar eclipses happen?

The Moon travels around Earth. A solar eclipse happens when the Moon comes between the Sun and the Earth and casts a huge shadow onto the Earth. A total eclipse is rare, but when it happens, the Sun seems to disappear from the sky and for a few moments everything becomes cold and dark.

THE SOLAR SYSTEM

SUN
MERCURY
VENUS
EARTH
MARS
JUPITER
SATURN

What is the solar system?

The solar system consists of the Sun and the planets that move around the Sun in oval paths called orbits. A planet is a vast ball of rock or gas that travels in orbit around a star. There are other objects in our solar system, too, such as moons and asteroids.

DID YOU KNOW?
The Sun is so far away that if you tried to drive there, traveling at 60 miles an hour, it would take you 170 years to reach your destination!

How far are we from the Sun?

Earth is 93 million miles away from the Sun. This means that our planet is far enough away from the Sun for water to be liquid. If Earth were closer and, therefore, warmer, water would turn to gas, and if it were farther away, water would become ice. It is Earth's distance from the Sun that makes it the only planet in the solar system that is known to support life.

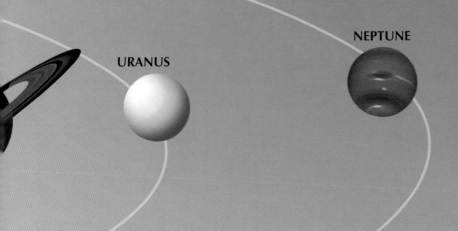

URANUS

NEPTUNE

PLUTO

These are the nine planets of our solar system. Earth is the third planet from the Sun.

Why do planets orbit the Sun?

The planets move around the Sun because the Sun is so big that its gravity is very powerful. Gravity is the force that pulls the planets toward the Sun. It is strong enough to hold all the planets in the solar system in their orbits, moving around the Sun in the same direction.

When did Earth form?

Earth and the other planets formed about five billion years ago. Our planet was born from dust and gases whirling in orbit around the Sun as it was forming. In the intense heat, the dust and gases collided and hardened into a ball of rock. Even today, the Earth is still hit by dust from space and the occasional large piece of rock.

13

THE ROCKY PLANETS

Which are the rocky planets?

Mercury, Venus, Earth, and Mars are known as the rocky planets because they are mainly made of rock and metal. Mercury is closest to the Sun. Although it is burning hot on this planet during the day, at night it becomes freezing cold. This is because Mercury's atmosphere is very thin and there are no clouds to trap and hold warmth during the night.

We cannot see the surface of Venus because it is always covered in thick clouds.

MERCURY

VENUS

Where is the hottest planet?

Although Venus is the second planet from the Sun, it has the hottest surface. It is hotter than Mercury because it has a blanket of fast-moving clouds around it. This traps heat from the Sun and stops the heat flowing out into space. The thick atmosphere on Venus is mostly made up of carbon dioxide gas, which would be deadly poisonous for people.

Why is Earth called the blue planet?

Earth is often called the blue planet, because three-quarters of its surface is covered in water and from space it looks blue. When the Earth formed, a layer of gas formed around it. This layer protects the Earth from getting too hot or too cold. Eventually, rain began to fall and formed our planet's rivers, lakes, and oceans.

DID YOU KNOW?
Some scientists believe there could be life on Mars. Although it is too cold for life to exist on the surface, tiny organisms could exist in warmer pockets below the ground.

EARTH

MARS

What makes Mars red?

Mars is known as the red planet because of the color of its soil. The surface of Mars is rich in iron oxide, which is rust and has a reddish color. Mars has little atmosphere and gets very cold. Like Earth, it has ice caps on its north pole and south pole but the rest of its surface is a dusty red desert.

THE GAS PLANETS

What are the gas planets?

Jupiter, Saturn, Uranus, and Neptune are known as the gas planets. These planets are large spinning balls of gas with small rocky cores (centers). Jupiter and Saturn are also known as the giant planets because they are so big. Jupiter is twice as heavy as all the other planets put together and Saturn is almost as large as Jupiter.

Jupiter is the largest planet in the solar system. The bright colors you can see are formed by the different gases in Jupiter's clouds.

BELOW Saturn's famous rings orbit around its middle. The rings are very thin compared to the size of the planet, none being more than 165 feet deep.

Why does Saturn have rings?

Saturn's rings are made up of dust and pieces of rock, and ice. Astronomers think that the dust and rock may have come from moons that broke up when they crashed into other objects in space. The millions of chunks of ice-covered rock that form the colorful rings are held in orbit around Saturn by the pull of the planet's gravity.

HOW many moons does Jupiter have?

Jupiter has 63 moons, and possibly more. A moon is an object that orbits around a planet. Some moons are rocky and round, but they can be icy or volcanic. Jupiter also has rings, like Saturn, but they are smaller and fainter. Uranus and Neptune have rings, too.

ABOVE If you look at Jupiter with binoculars, you can easily see its four main moons. Italian astronomer Galileo Galilei was the first person to see these moons, along with Saturn's rings, in 1610, using an early telescope.

DID YOU KNOW?

Some of the billions of pieces of dust, rock, and ice that make up Saturn's rings are as big as a house. Others are as small as grains of sand.

When were Uranus, Neptune, and Pluto discovered?

Astronomers discovered Uranus, Neptune, and Pluto later than the other planets because these planets are so far away. Uranus was found in 1781, Neptune in 1846, and Pluto, which is five times smaller than Earth, in 1930. Pluto is so small that astronomers argue it is not a planet at all. It is also so far away that no maps have yet been made of its surface.

URANUS

PLUTO

NEPTUNE

ASTEROIDS, COMETS, AND METEORS

What is a comet?

A comet is a lump of rock, ice, and frozen gas that orbits around the Sun. A comet remains icy and frozen while its orbit carries it far from the Sun. When it gets closer to the Sun, the frozen gas and dust evaporate and form a glowing tail that can stretch for millions of miles.

Gas tail

Comet

When can we see Halley's Comet?

The most famous comet, Halley's Comet, can be seen every 76 years and will reappear in 2061. People have been observing this comet for more than 2,000 years. It was named after English astronomer Edmond Halley, who, in 1682, realized the comet had been seen before. About 20 different comets can be seen from Earth each year. Most of these are faint and can only be seen with a telescope.

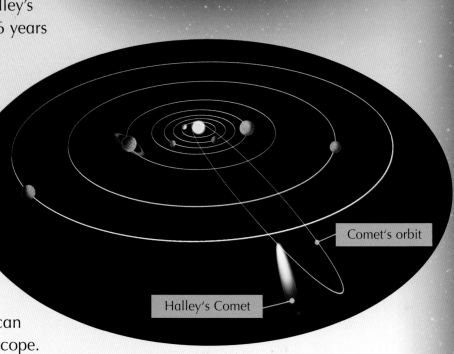

Comet's orbit

Halley's Comet

How big is an asteroid?

Asteroids are oddly shaped
rocks that travel in orbit
around the Sun. They range
in size from tiny particles to
huge lumps nearly
600 miles across. Most
asteroids are found in what
is known as the Asteroid
Belt, between Mars and
Jupiter. Others travel in
an orbit closer to the Sun.
Some have been pulled into
the orbits of planets, such
as Jupiter, Mars, and Earth,
by these planets' gravity.

Where do meteorites come from?

Meteorites are pieces of rock that come from outer
space. When they reach Earth, they usually burn up in
the atmosphere, where they can be seen as as streaks
of light called meteors. The few that make it through
Earth's atmosphere and hit the surface are meteorites.
Most are the size of pebbles, but, long ago, huge
meteorites made vast craters in Earth's surface.

THE MOON

How big is the Moon?

The Moon is about a quarter of the size of Earth and measures 2,160 miles wide. The Moon is Earth's only natural satellite and is held in orbit by the pull of Earth's gravity. It takes the Moon about four weeks to complete one orbit of the Earth. Our word "month," which means a period of about four weeks, comes from the word "Moon."

BELOW Scientists believe that there are large amounts of frozen water hidden in craters on the Moon's surface. A crater appears as a dark shadow on the Moon's surface.

Crater

Sea

Why is the Moon covered in craters?

The Moon's atmosphere is very thin and gives no protection against rocks from space that smash into the surface. These impacts create large dips called craters. Some craters are huge and were made by rocks as big as mountains. Most of the Moon's surface is covered in dust. There are also parts called "seas" that are not water but dried lava that poured from volcanoes long ago.

Crescent Moon   Full Moon   Crescent Moon

What are the Moon's phases?

The different shapes the Moon appears to take throughout the month are called the phases of the Moon. When we see the whole Moon, we call it a Full Moon. When we cannot see the Moon at all, we call it a New Moon. When we can see only a thin sliver of the Moon, we call it a crescent Moon. The Moon doesn't change shape—we just see different parts of it when it is in different stages of its orbit around Earth.

ABOVE These are the Moon's phases as we see them throughout the month. The Moon's shape changes from a thin crescent to a circle and back again.

Who was the first person on the Moon?

American astronaut Neil Armstrong was the first person on the Moon. As he left his landing craft on July 21, 1969, he said, "That's one small step for man but one giant leap for mankind." He and fellow astronaut Edwin "Buzz" Aldrin collected soil samples and took photos. The Moon's weak gravity made it easy to move around, but they had to wear space suits because there is no air there and the Sun's light is very strong.

DISCOVERING SPACE

Where is the world's biggest telescope?

The biggest telescopes in the world are at the Keck Observatories on the top of an extinct volcano in Hawaii. These two optical telescopes use mirrors instead of lenses to gather faint light from faraway galaxies. The main mirror in each telescope measures 33 feet across.

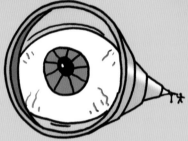

DID YOU KNOW?
Astronomers are planning to build bigger and bigger optical telescopes, with mirrors that are 100 to 300 feet wide.

Why do we need space telescopes?

When astronomers look through telescopes based on the Earth they have to look through our planet's cloudy, dusty atmosphere into space. Space telescopes sit above the atmosphere so that they can see into space more clearly. The Hubble Space Telescope orbits at about 375 miles above the Earth. It has given astronomers incredibly clear views of our own solar system and faraway galaxies.

LEFT The Hubble Space Telescope was launched in 1990.

How do space probes work?

Space probes are small, robot craft that are launched into space. They are programmed to fly past planets or land on them. Probes take photographs and use radar and other equipment to gather information. Then they send this information back to Earth using radio signals. In 2004, a NASA probe landed on Mars and sent back astonishing new pictures of the planet's surface.

What happens in a space station?

A space station is like a laboratory in space where astronauts study stars and other objects, and measure the way in which things, such as weightlessness, affect people. Astronauts travel to and from a space station on other spacecraft, and they live and work on board for weeks at a time. In addition to research laboratories and equipment, such as telescopes, a space station has living and eating quarters for the astronauts.

OUR EARTH

Mantle

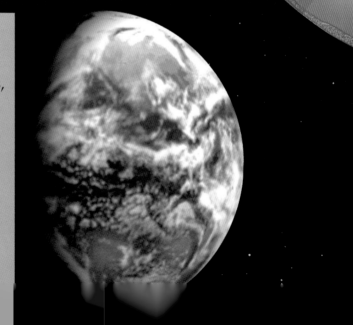

Why does Earth have seasons?

Earth has seasons because it is tilted at an angle. This means that as it orbits around the Sun different parts are tilted toward the Sun. When the northern hemisphere, or top half of the Earth, points to the Sun, this area gets summer. At the same time, the southern hemisphere, or bottom half of the Earth, is pointing away from the Sun and this area experiences its winter.

LEFT · Seen here is the same meadow in summer (top), fall (middle), and winter (bottom).

What causes night and day?

Night and day happen because Earth rotates, or makes one complete turn, every 24 hours. In addition to traveling in an orbit around the Sun, planet Earth spins around its axis, an imaginary line going through the North and South Poles. This means that at any one time, half of Earth is facing the Sun and is in daylight, while the other half faces away from the Sun, so is in night-time.

Outer core

What is inside the Earth?

Inside the center of the Earth there is red-hot, liquid rock. This rock is called magma. The land and oceans at the Earth's surface lie on an outer layer of cool, hard rock called the crust. The hot magma below rises and sinks slowly in a layer called the mantle. At the very center of the Earth is a superhot ball of iron called the core.

DID YOU KNOW?
The Earth's surface is cracked into large pieces, called plates, which fit together like an enormous jigsaw puzzle. There are nine large plates and several smaller ones.

Crust

Core

60 million years ago

155 million years ago

How did the land divide into continents?

The land sits on top of the large pieces, or plates, that make up the Earth's surface. These plates are slowly moving. Before about 200 million years ago, all the land was joined to form one big continent, called a supercontinent. Over millions of years, as the plates moved, the land split and slowly divided into the seven continents we know today: Africa, Antarctica, Asia, Australia, Europe, North America, and South America.

200 million years ago

MOUNTAINS AND VALLEYS

How do mountains form?

Some mountains form from volcanoes. Dome mountains occur where magma near the Earth's surface forms a rounded bulge of rock but does not erupt to become a volcano. Fold mountains form when two colliding plates cause the Earth's crust to buckle and fold, making mountain ranges. Block mountains form when fractures in the Earth's crust push a block of rock upward.

Do mountains continue to grow?

Yes, some mountains continue to get taller after they first form! For example, the Himalayas are growing by just over 2 inches every year. The Himalayas were formed 50 million years ago when two of the Earth's plates collided. As the plates continue to push into each other the mountains are gradually getting higher—and they are getting even harder to climb!

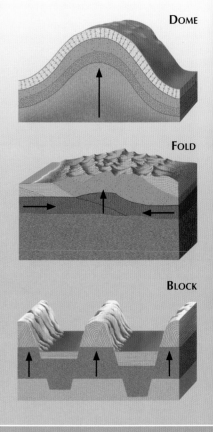

DOME

FOLD

BLOCK

DID YOU KNOW?
The Mid-Atlantic Ocean Ridge is an underwater mountain range. It is as long as the Rocky, Andes, and Himalaya mountain ranges combined.

What is a glacier?

A glacier is a huge river of ice. A buildup of snow and ice in very cold, high mountain areas causes the river of ice to flow downhill. Most glaciers flow so slowly you cannot tell they are moving. As glaciers move, they carry rocks along with them that help gouge out valleys, or deep grooves, into the land through which they pass.

Mountain glaciers have created many of the valleys on the Earth's surface.

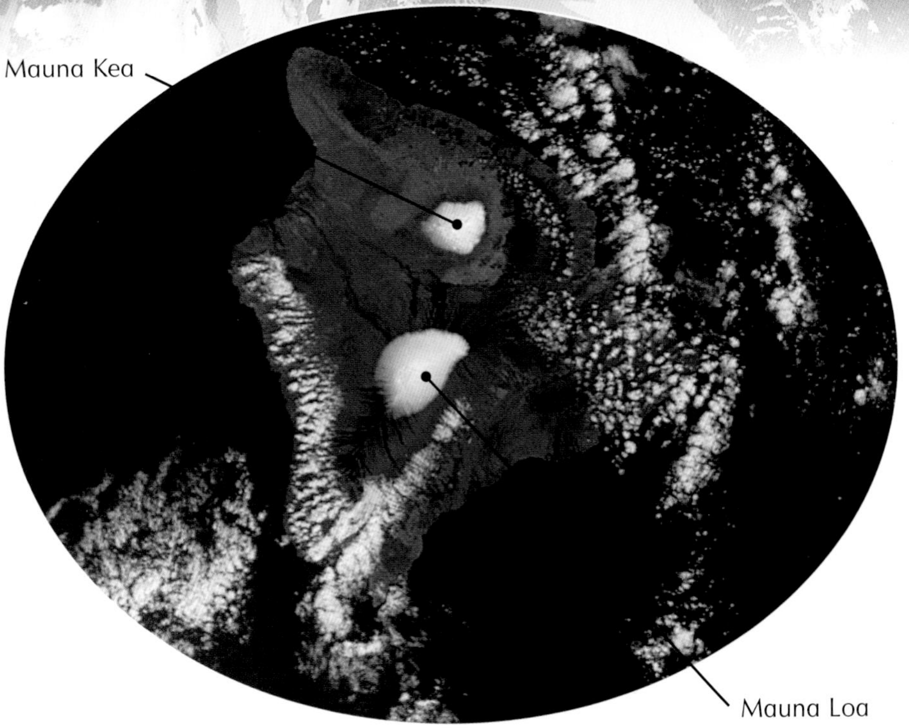

Mauna Kea

Mauna Loa

Where is the tallest mountain?

The tallest mountain is Mauna Kea on Hawaii. It measures 33,375 feet from base to peak, but most of it is underwater. Only 13,795 feet of it are above sea level. On land, Mount Everest is the highest mountain, reaching 29,035 feet above sea level. Also on Hawaii is Mauna Loa, the world's biggest volcano.

SHAPING THE EARTH

What is weathering?

Weathering is the wearing away of rock at the Earth's surface. Weathering can be caused by wind, frost, rain, and heat from the Sun. Weathering can even change the shape of mountains. When rain seeps into cracks in rocks it may turn to ice. Ice takes up more space than water and the ice makes the cracks bigger. Eventually, weathering breaks off whole pieces of rock and they fall away.

BELOW The Grand Canyon is 275 miles long. In places, it is 15 miles wide and over 1 mile deep.

How was the Grand Canyon formed?

The Grand Canyon in Arizona is the largest valley on Earth and was created by water. The force and weight of the water shape the land through which a river flows. The water wears away pieces of rock and these pieces help the river scratch away deeper into the land. This is how the Colorado River gradually carved out the Grand Canyon over many centuries.

When do sand dunes form?

Sand dunes form when the wind blows small, light grains of sand into hills and mounds along coastlines and in deserts. Sand is made when rocks are weathered by wind and water. As stones are tossed together in the water, or blown into each other by the wind, they gradually break up. They get smaller and smaller, until eventually they become grains of sand.

Why is the coastline shrinking?

Coastlines all around the world are shrinking because of the power of the sea. As waves crash against shorelines, they wear away rocks at the bottom of cliffs. When these rocks break away, the upper part of the cliff falls into the sea, too. The waves crash these pieces of rock together and break them into small pieces that the water washes away.

DID YOU KNOW?
In some places, many years of weathering has worn away entire mountains.

31

THE EARTH'S ATMOSPHERE

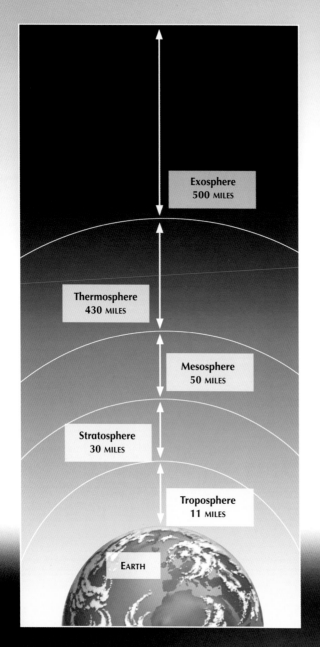

Exosphere	500 MILES
Thermosphere	430 MILES
Mesosphere	50 MILES
Stratosphere	30 MILES
Troposphere	11 MILES
EARTH	

Where is the atmosphere?

The atmosphere is the layer of air that surrounds the Earth. It is like a blanket of gases wrapped around the planet. One of the most important gases in the atmosphere is oxygen, which all living things need to live. The atmosphere protects the Earth by filtering out harmful rays from the Sun. The atmosphere is divided into smaller layers. The nearest one to the Earth is the troposphere.

What is air pressure?

Air pressure is the weight of the air in the atmosphere that presses down on the Earth. The amount of air pressure varies at different places on the Earth. If you are up a mountain, there is less air above you, so the air pressure is less. We do not usually feel the weight of the air pressing down on us because air within our bodies pushes out, balancing the pressure with the air outside.

ABOVE Mountaineers sometimes carry oxygen bottles because the air is thinner and it can be harder to breathe high up a mountain.

How does the greenhouse effect work?

Some gases in the atmosphere are known as greenhouse gases because they keep our planet warm, similar to the way greenhouse glass keeps plants inside warm. When heat from the Sun hits the Earth, much of it bounces back into the sky. Greenhouse gases stop the Sun's warmth from escaping into space and reflect the heat back to the Earth.

Sun

Atmosphere

Some of the Sun's rays are reflected back into space or absorbed by the atmosphere.

Some of the Sun's rays hit the Earth.

Some heat bounces back to Earth.

Some heat escapes into space.

DID YOU KNOW?
Without the greenhouse gases in the atmosphere, heat would escape back into space and Earth's average temperature would be about 95 degrees Fahrenheit colder.

Why is global warming a problem?

Global warming is an increase in world temperatures caused by the greenhouse effect. It is a problem because the extra heat in the atmosphere leads to more severe weather, such as storms and floods. The heat also causes polar ice to melt, leading to rising sea levels. Humans are contributing to the problem by burning fuels that pump more greenhouse gases into the atmosphere.

Ancient Egypt ›

The ancient Egyptian civilization grew up along the Nile River, in northeastern Africa, from about 3150 BC. Under the rule of kings known as pharaohs, the Egyptians made great strides in building, art, and science.

› HOW OLD ARE THE PYRAMIDS?

The first pyramid was built between 2630 and 2611 BC. It had stepped sides and was built for King Djoser. Before then, pharaohs were buried in flat-top mounds called mastabas. The last pyramid in Egypt itself was built around 1530 BC.

› WHY WERE THE PYRAMIDS BUILT?

The pyramids are huge tombs for pharaohs and nobility. The Egyptians believed that dead people's spirits could live on after death if their bodies were carefully preserved. It was especially important to preserve the bodies of dead pharaohs because their spirits would help the kingdom of Egypt to survive. So they made dead bodies into mummies, and buried them in these splendid tombs along with clothes and jewels.

PYRAMID OF KHAFRE

Pharaoh Khafre's pyramid was completed in about 2530 BC in Giza, near Cairo.

➤ HOW WAS A PYRAMID BUILT?

By manpower! Thousands of laborers worked in the hot sun to clear the site, lay the foundations, drag building stone from the quarry, and lift it into place. Most of the laborers were ordinary farmers, who worked as builders to pay their dues to the pharaoh. Expert craftsmen cut the stone into blocks and fitted them together.

➤ WHY DID EGYPTIANS TREASURE SCARABS?

Scarabs (beetles) collect animal dung and roll it into little balls. To the Egyptians, these dung balls looked like the life-giving sun, so they hoped that scarabs would bring them long life.

➤ HOW WERE CORPSES MUMMIFIED?

Making a mummy was a complicated and expensive process. First, most of the soft internal organs were removed, then the body was packed in chemicals and left to dry out. Finally, it was wrapped in resin-soaked linen bandages, and placed in a beautifully decorated coffin.

WHY WAS THE NILE RIVER SO IMPORTANT?

Because Egypt got almost no rain. But every year the Nile flooded the fields along its banks, bringing fresh water and rich black silt, which helped crops to grow. Farmers dug irrigation channels to carry water to distant fields. All of Egypt's great cities lay on the river, which was also a vital thoroughfare for boats carrying people and goods.

FELUCCA

Wooden boats called feluccas have sailed on the Nile for millennia.

MUMMY

After embalming, a body was wrapped in a sheet and placed in a coffin to keep it safe.

Vikings >

The Vikings came from Norway, Denmark, and Sweden. Starting from around AD 800 until AD 1100, these warriors made raids across Europe, killing, burning, and carrying away all that they could manage.

> WERE THE VIKINGS GOOD SAILORS?

Yes. They sailed for thousands of miles across the icy northern oceans in open wooden boats, known as longboats. They learned how to navigate by observing the sun and the stars.

LONGBOAT

A reconstruction of a Viking longboat shows the streamlined, lightweight design.

> WHAT GODS DID THE VIKINGS BELIEVE IN?

The Vikings prayed to many different gods. Thor sent thunder and protected craftsmen. Odin was the god of wisdom and war. Kindly goddess Freya gave peace and fruitful crops.

> WHAT WERE VIKING SHIPS MADE OF?

Narrow, flexible strips of wood, attached to a solid wooden backbone called a keel. Viking warships were long and narrow, and could sail very fast. They were powered by men rowing, or by the wind trapped in big square sails.

❯ DID THE VIKINGS REACH NORTH AMERICA?

Yes, around AD 1000. A bold adventurer named Leif Ericsson sailed westward from Greenland until he reached "Vinland" (present-day Newfoundland, Canada). He built a farmstead there, but quarreled with the local people, and decided to return home.

LEIF ERICSSON

This adventurer was based in a Viking colony in Greenland.

❯ WHAT DOES "VIKING" MEAN?

The word "Viking" comes from the old Scandinavian word *vik*, which means "a narrow bay by the sea." That's where the Vikings lived. It was hard to make a living in the cold Viking homelands, so Viking men raided wealthier lands. But not all Vikings were raiders. Some traveled to new places to settle, and many were hunters and farmers who never left home.

WHAT DID VIKINGS SEIZE ON THEIR RAIDS?

All kinds of treasure. A hoard of silver (below), including coins and belt buckles, was buried by Vikings in the tenth century and discovered by workmen in Lancashire, England, in 1840. The Vikings also kidnapped people to sell as slaves.

Aztecs, Maya, and Incas >

Before the Spanish conquest of the Americas in the sixteenth century, Central and South America were home to some of the world's greatest civilizations. Beautiful cities and pyramids were built, while scholars studied astronomy and mathematics.

> ## WHO WERE THE INCAS?

A people who lived in the Andes Mountains of South America (part of present-day Peru and Ecuador). They ruled a mighty empire from the early fifteenth century to early sixteenth century AD.

MACHU PICCHU

This Inca city was built of polished stone around AD 1460.

➤ WHO BUILT PYRAMIDS TO STUDY THE STARS?

Priests of the Maya civilization, which was powerful in Central America between AD 200 and 900. They built huge, stepped pyramids, with temples and observatories at the top. The Maya were expert astronomers and mathematicians, and worked out very accurate calendars.

CHICHEN ITZA

The step pyramid is topped by a temple dedicated to the Maya serpent god Kukulkan.

➤ WHO WERE THE AZTECS?

The Aztecs were wandering hunters who arrived in Mexico about AD 1200. They fought against the people already living there, built a city called Tenochtitlán on an island in a marshy lake, and soon grew rich and strong.

➤ WHO WROTE IN PICTURES?

Maya and Aztec scribes. The Maya used a system of picture symbols called glyphs. Maya and Aztecs both wrote in stitched books, called codices, using paper made from the bark of a fig tree.

➤ HOW DID THE MAYA, AZTECS, AND INCAS LOSE THEIR POWER?

They were conquered by soldiers from Spain, who arrived in the Americas in the early sixteenth century, looking for treasure, especially gold.

TOP ? QUESTION

WHY WERE LLAMAS SO IMPORTANT?

Because they could survive in the Incas' mountain homeland, over 10,000 feet above sea level. It is cold and windy there, and few plants grow. The Incas wove cloth from llama wool, and used llamas to carry loads up steep mountain paths.

43

The Islamic world →

Between about AD 700 and 1200, the Islamic world experienced a period of great power. It led the rest of the globe in learning, invention, and architecture. Islamic leaders controlled lands from southern Spain to northwest India.

› WHAT IS ISLAM?

The religious faith taught by the Prophet Muhammad. People who follow the faith of Islam are called Muslims. Muhammad was a religious leader who lived in Arabia from AD 570 to 632. He taught people to worship Allah, the one God. At its peak, the vast Islamic World—stretching from Spain and North Africa, through Central Asia to northwest India—was ruled by Muslim princes and governed by Islamic laws.

› WHO WERE THE MONGOLS?

They were nomads who roamed across Central Asia. In AD 1206, the Mongol tribes united under a leader known as Genghis Khan ("Supreme Ruler") and set out to conquer the world. At its peak, the Mongol Empire spread from China to eastern Europe.

LA MEZQUITA

The Muslim rulers of Spain built a great mosque in the city of Córdoba starting from AD 784.

➤ WHO INVENTED THE ASTROLABE?

The astrolabe was perfected by Muslim scientists who lived and worked in the Middle East in the eighth century. Astrolabes were scientific instruments that helped sailors find their position when they were at sea. They worked by measuring the height of the sun above the horizon.

➤ WHO LIVED IN A CIRCULAR CITY?

The citizens of Baghdad, which was founded in AD 762 by the caliph (ruler) al-Mansur. He employed builders and architects to create a huge circular city, surrounded by strong walls. There were palaces, government offices, mosques, hospitals, schools, libraries, and gardens.

ASTROLABE

Astrolabes can be used for navigation and timekeeping.

➤ WHAT WERE SHIPS OF THE DESERT?

Camels owned by merchants who lived in Arabia. They were the only animals that could survive long enough without food and water to make journeys across the desert, laden with goods to sell. They stored enough nourishment in their humps to last several days.

TOP ? QUESTION

WHAT WERE THE CRUSADES?

A series of wars fought between Christian and Muslim soldiers for control of the area around Jerusalem (in present-day Israel), which was holy to Muslims, Christians, and Jews. The Crusades began in 1095, when a Christian army attacked (right). Their main period ended in 1291, when Muslim soldiers forced the Christians to leave.

China and Japan

China was one of the earliest centers of human civilization, with its first cities founded more than 4,000 years ago. On the islands of Japan, people were making decorated pottery an amazing 12,000 years ago. Pottery found there is among the oldest in the world.

WHAT MADE CHINA SO RICH?

The inventions of Chinese farmers and engineers made the land productive. In the Middle Ages, the Chinese made spectacular strides in agriculture. They dug networks of irrigation channels to bring water to the rice fields. They built machines, such as a foot-powered pump to lift water to the fields. The emperor and government officials also ruled China very effectively, allowing it to grow wealthy.

HOW DID CHINA GET ITS NAME?

From the Qin (pronounced "chin") dynasty, the first dynasty to rule over a united China. Founded by Ch'in Shih Huang Ti, China's first emperor, it lasted from 221 to 206 BC. It was responsible for the standardization of Chinese script, weights and measures, and the construction of the Great Wall.

GOLDEN TEMPLE

The temple was built in the fourteenth century in Kyoto, Japan.

WHERE WAS THE MIDDLE KINGDOM?

The Chinese believed their country was at the center of the world, so they called it the Middle Kingdom. In fact, for centuries, China was one of the most advanced civilizations on earth. Under the Tang and Song dynasties (AD 618–1279) Chinese cities, such as Chang'an (modern Xi'an), were the world's biggest.

FORBIDDEN CITY

Built from 1406, the palace, "forbidden" to outsiders, was home to China's emperors.

INNER COURT

A walkway leads to the Palace of Heavenly Purity, where the emperor received guests.

WHAT WAS CHINA'S BEST-KEPT SECRET?

How to make silk. For centuries, no one else knew how. Chinese women fed silk-moth grubs on mulberry leaves, and the grubs spun thread and wrapped themselves in it to make cocoons. Workers steamed the cocoons to kill the grubs, unwound the thread, dyed it, and wove it into cloth.

WHO VALUED HONOR MORE THAN LIFE?

Japanese warriors, called samurai, who were powerful starting from around the twelfth century. They were taught to fight according to a strict code of honor. They believed that it was better to commit suicide than to face defeat.

WHICH RULERS CLAIMED DESCENT FROM THE SUN GODDESS?

The emperors of Japan. The first Japanese emperor lived around 660 BC. His descendants ruled until AD 1192. After that, shoguns (army generals) ran the government, leaving the emperors with only religious and ceremonial powers.

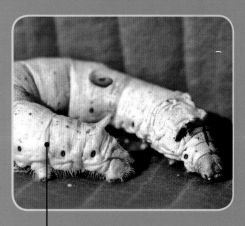

SILKWORM

Silkworms have been kept in China for at least 5,000 years.

Europe >

After the Roman Empire released its hold on the rest of Europe, the countries of Europe were ruled by kings, queens, and nobles. As they farmed the land, many ordinary people lived in great poverty.

> WHEN WERE THE MIDDLE AGES?

When historians refer to the Middle Ages, or the medieval period, they usually mean the time from the collapse of the Roman Empire, around AD 500, to about AD 1500.

> WHO FARMED LAND THEY DID NOT OWN?

Poor peasant families. Under medieval law, all the land belonged to the king, or to rich nobles. The peasants lived in little cottages in return for rent or for work on the land. Sometimes the peasants protested or tried to run away.

> WHO DID BATTLE IN METAL SUITS?

Kings, lords, and knights who lived in Europe during the Middle Ages. In those days, men from aristocratic families were brought up to fight and lead soldiers into battle. It was their duty, according to law. From around AD 1000, knights wore simple chain-mail tunics, but by about 1450, armor was made of shaped metal plates, carefully pieced together. The most expensive suits of armor were decorated with engraved patterns or polished gold.

ARMOR

Medieval armor covered the body from head to toe.

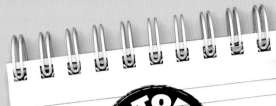

WHO BUILT CASTLES AND CATHEDRALS?

Kings, queens, and nobles. The first castles were wooden forts. Later, they were built of stone. Cathedrals were very big churches in cities or towns. They were built to reflect God's glory and to bring honor to those who had paid for them.

➤ WHO WAS THE VIRGIN QUEEN?

Elizabeth I of England (above), who reigned from 1558 to 1603, at a time when many people believed that women were too weak to rule. Elizabeth proved them wrong. Under her leadership, England grew stronger. She never married and ruled alone.

NOTRE DAME

The Bishop of Paris ordered the construction of the cathedral in 1163.

➤ WHICH RUSSIAN CZAR WAS TERRIBLE?

Ivan IV, who was known as Ivan the Terrible. He became czar, or emperor, in 1533, when he was three years old. He was clever but ruthless, and killed everyone who opposed him. He passed laws removing many of the rights of peasants, making them almost serfs, like slaves.

Africa and India ➤

By the Middle Ages, African cities were rich centers of learning and trade, with merchants traveling as far afield as India and Southeast Asia. And throughout its long history, India has been home to many great empires, from the Mauryans (322–185 BC) to the Mughals.

➤ WHERE DID DHOWS SAIL TO TRADE?

Dhows were ships built for rich merchants living in trading ports, such as Kilwa, in East Africa. They sailed to the Red Sea and the Persian Gulf to buy pearls and perfumes, across the Indian Ocean to India to buy silks and jewels, and to Malaysia and Indonesia to buy spices.

➤ WHICH AFRICAN CITY HAD A FAMOUS UNIVERSITY?

Timbuktu, in present-day Mali, West Africa. The city was founded in the eleventh century and became a great center of learning for Muslim scholars from many lands. Timbuktu also had several mosques and markets, a royal palace, and a library.

DHOW

A traditional wooden dhow is powered by triangular-shaped sails.

➤ WHICH KINGS BUILT TALL TOWERS?

Shona kings of southeast Africa, who built a city called Great Zimbabwe. Zimbabwe means "stone houses." The city was also a massive fortress. From inside this fortress, the Shona kings ruled a rich empire from AD 1100 to 1600.

❯ WHO FOUNDED A NEW RELIGION IN INDIA?

Guru Nanak, a religious teacher who lived in northwest India from 1469 to 1539. He taught that there is one God, and that people should respect one another equally, as brothers and sisters. His followers became known as Sikhs.

❯ HOW LONG DID THE MUGHALS RULE INDIA?

For more than three centuries, starting from 1526 until 1858. The Mughal dynasty was descended from the great Mongol warrior Genghis Khan (Mughal is a north Indian way of writing Mongol). The last Mughal emperor was toppled when the British government took control of India.

GOLDEN TEMPLE OF AMRITSAR

The beautiful temple, begun in 1574, is one of the most important places of worship for Sikhs.

TAJ MAHAL

To construct the building, 20,000 workers were recruited from as far afield as Persia and Syria.

❯ WHO BUILT THE TAJ MAHAL?

The Mughal emperor Shah Jehan (ruled 1628–58). He was so sad when his wife Mumtaz Mahal died that he built a lovely tomb for her, called the Taj Mahal. It is made of pure white marble decorated with gold and semiprecious stones.

Pacific Ocean lands

Australia, New Zealand, and the Polynesian islands lie in the Pacific Ocean. They were probably first colonized by voyagers from Southeast Asia. From the sixteenth century, Europeans started to explore the Pacific lands.

WHO WAS THE FIRST TO SAIL AROUND THE WORLD?

It was sailors in the ship *Victoria*, owned by Ferdinand Magellan, a Portuguese explorer. In 1519, he sailed westward from Europe, but was killed fighting in the Philippines. His captain, Sebastian Elcano, managed to complete the voyage, and returned home to Europe, weak but triumphant, in 1522.

HOW DID SAILORS HELP SCIENCE?

European sailors often observed the plants, fish, and animals as they traveled, and brought specimens home with them. When Captain James Cook explored the Pacific Ocean, he took artists and scientists with him to record what they saw.

CAPTAIN COOK

This drawing was made by Captain Cook's official artist, John Webber, when the expedition arrived in Hawaii in 1799.

DID THE ABORIGINALS ALWAYS LIVE IN AUSTRALIA?

No, they probably arrived from Southeast Asia about 60,000 years ago, when the sea around Australia was shallower than today. They may have traveled by land or in small boats. It is believed that the Aboriginal settlers introduced dogs to Australia—the ancestors of today's dingoes. They were used as guard and hunting dogs, and to keep Aboriginal people warm as they slept around campfires in the desert, which is cold at night.

➤ WHO WERE THE FIRST PEOPLE TO DISCOVER NEW ZEALAND?

The Maoris. They began a mass migration from other Pacific Islands at around AD 1150, but remains dating back to AD 800 have been found in New Zealand.

MAORI CARVING

Wood carving—on buildings and decorative items—is an important part of traditional Maori culture.

➤ HOW DID THE POLYNESIAN PEOPLE CROSS THE PACIFIC OCEAN?

By sailing and paddling big outrigger canoes. They steered by studying the waves and the stars, and made maps out of twigs and shells to help themselves navigate.

POLYNESIAN CANOE

The canoe has an outrigger, or support, on one side for stability.

North America >

The earliest evidence for the settlement of North America dates from 14,000 years ago. These ancestors of today's Native Americans were farmers, hunters, and traders. The first Europeans to settle in North America arrived in the mid-sixteenth century.

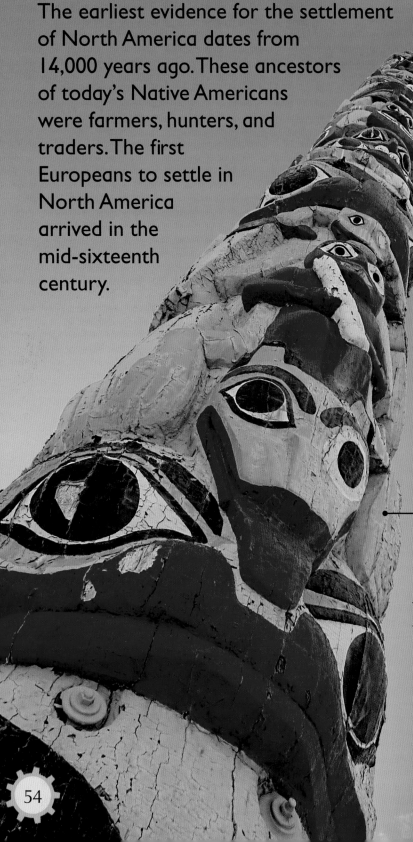

> WHAT STORIES DO TOTEM POLES TELL?

Native American people who lived in the forests of northwest North America carved tall totem poles to record their family's history, and to retell ancient legends about the powerful spirits that lived in all rocks, mountains, wild animals, and trees.

> WHO LIVED IN TENTS ON THE GREAT PLAINS?

Native American hunters, such as the Sioux and the Cheyenne. After Europeans settled in North America, bringing horses with them, Native Americans spent summer on the grasslands of the Great Plains, following herds of buffalo, which they killed for meat and skins. In winter, they camped in sheltered valleys. Before the Europeans brought horses, Native Americans were mainly farmers.

TOTEM POLE

The word "totem" comes from the Ojibwe people of Canada's word for family or tribe.

> WHY DID THE PILGRIMS LEAVE HOME?

The Pilgrims were a group of English families with strong religious beliefs, who quarreled with Church leaders and the government. In 1620, they sailed in the *Mayflower* to North America, to build a new community where they could practice their religion in peace.

➤ WHEN DID THE USA BECOME INDEPENDENT?

On July 4, 1776, 13 English colonies (where most Europeans in North America had settled) made a Declaration of Independence, refusing to be ruled by Britain any longer. They became a new nation, the United States of America. Britain sent more troops to win the colonies back, but was defeated in 1783.

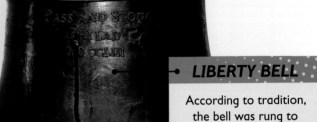

LIBERTY BELL

According to tradition, the bell was rung to announce the Declaration of Independence in 1776.

➤ WHO WERE THE FIRST EUROPEANS TO SETTLE IN NORTH AMERICA?

Spanish colonists, who settled in present-day Florida and California, beginning around 1540. An English settlement began in Jamestown, Virginia, in 1607 and in Massachusetts in 1620.

WHY DID A CIVIL WAR BREAK OUT?

The Civil War (1861–65), between the northern and southern states, was caused mainly by a quarrel over slavery. The southern states relied on African slaves working in their cotton plantations. The northern states wanted slavery banned. After four years, the northern states won, and slavery was abolished.

The Industrial Revolution >

The Industrial Revolution was a huge change in the way people worked and goods were produced. Machines in large factories replaced craftspeople working by hand. It began around 1775 in Britain and spread slowly to the United States and other countries in Europe.

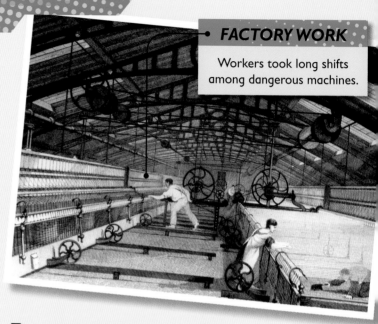

❯ WHEN DID THE FIRST TRAINS RUN?

Horse-drawn railroad wagons had been used to haul coal and stone from mines and quarries since the sixteenth century, but the first passenger railroad was opened by George Stephenson in the north of England in 1825. Its locomotives were powered by steam.

❯ WHO WORKED IN THE FIRST FACTORIES?

Thousands of poor men and women moved from the countryside to live in fast-growing factory towns. They hoped to find regular work and more pay. Wages in factories were better than those on farms, but factories were often dirty and dangerous.

STEPHENSON'S ROCKET

In 1829, George Stephenson built a groundbreaking steam locomotive, called the *Rocket*.

➤ DID CHILDREN LEAD BETTER LIVES THEN?

No. Many worked 16 hours a day in factories and mines. Large numbers were killed in accidents with machinery, or died from breathing coal dust or chemical fumes. After 1802, governments began to pass laws to protect child workers.

➤ WHY WERE DRAINS AND TOILETS SO IMPORTANT?

Because without them, diseases carried in sewage could spread quickly in crowded industrial towns. Pottery making was one of the first mass-production industries—and the factories made thousands of toilets!

➤ HOW DID THE RAILROADS CHANGE PEOPLE'S LIVES?

They helped trade and industry to grow by carrying raw materials to factories, and finished goods from factories to stores. They carried fresh foods from farms to cities. They made it easier for people to travel and encouraged a whole new vacation industry.

WHY WAS STEAM POWER SO IMPORTANT?

The development of the steam engine was one of the key breakthroughs that allowed the Industrial Revolution to take place. A steam engine can do work—such as powering machines or trains—using hot steam. Steam power allowed quicker production of goods in factories (below) and then their swift transportation to buyers.

The Modern Age ⟩

Since 1900, the world has changed in many ways. Women now play an important part in government. Technology has revolutionized our lives. But wars and poverty still blight the world.

⟩ WHAT WAS THE LONG MARCH?

A grueling march across China, covering 5,000 miles, made by around 100,000 Communists escaping their enemies. They were led by Mao Tse-tung, who became ruler of China in 1949.

⟩ WHO FOUGHT AND DIED IN THE TRENCHES?

Millions of young men during World War I (1914–18). Trenches were ditches dug into the ground. They were meant to shelter soldiers from gunfire, but offered little protection from shells exploding overhead. Soon, the trenches filled up with mud, water, rats, and dead bodies.

TOP QUESTION **?**

WHO DROPPED THE FIRST ATOMIC BOMB?

On August 6, 1945, the United States bombed Hiroshima in Japan, killing 66,000 people instantly. Two-thirds of the city's buildings were destroyed (right). Days later, Japan surrendered, ending World War II.

WHAT WAS THE COLD WAR?

A time of dangerous tension from the 1940s to the 1980s between the United States and the USSR, the two strongest nations in the world. The United States believed in democracy and capitalism; the USSR was Communist—and the countries distrusted one another. The superpowers never fought face to face, but their enmity drew them into local conflicts around the globe.

MAN ON THE MOON

The American astronaut Buzz Aldrin (left) was the second man to set foot on the Moon. The first man on the Moon was his companion Neil Armstrong, who took this famous photo.

WHO TOOK PART IN THE SPACE RACE?

The USSR and the United States. Each tried to rival the other's achievements in space. The USSR took the lead by launching the first satellite in 1957, but the Americans won the race by landing the first man on the Moon in 1969.

PEOPLE AND PLACES

AROUND THE WORLD

How many people are there in the world?

There are more than 6.5 billion people in the world! Many people today have more food and better health care than they had in the past and so they live longer than before. As more people live longer, the number of children being born is higher than the number of people who die. This means that the planet's population is increasing.

DID YOU KNOW?
The smallest country in the world is the Vatican City in Rome, Italy. It only covers a total area of about 100 acres—about the size of 50 football fields.

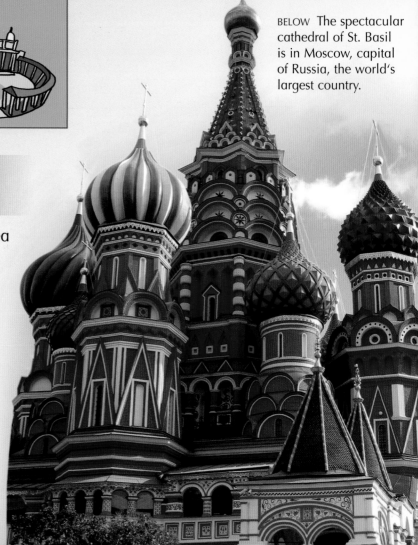

BELOW The spectacular cathedral of St. Basil is in Moscow, capital of Russia, the world's largest country.

Which are the world's largest countries?

The world's largest countries by area are Russia, Canada, the United States, and China. The largest is Russia—it is almost twice the size of Canada. Russia has a variety of landscapes, from vast plains to mountain ranges. Russia's Lake Baikal, the world's deepest lake, contains one-fifth of the Earth's fresh water.

Which country has the most people?

The country with the largest population in the world is China. Over 1.3 billion people live here. Most are Chinese but there are 55 different ethnic groups altogether. Since the 1970s, China has tried to slow down its population growth by encouraging couples to have just one child. By 2030 India, which has over a billion people, will probably have a larger population than China.

LEFT Chinese cities, such as Shanghai, are among the world's wealthiest and fastest-growing cities.

When do new countries form?

Sometimes a new country forms when two or more separate countries join together. Some new countries form when an area becomes independent of a larger country and starts to rule itself. This happened in the 1990s when Yugoslavia began splitting into separate countries (left). In the past, some countries conquered other lands and ruled over them as part of an empire. When the empires collapsed these lands became new independent countries.

63

WHERE PEOPLE LIVE

KEY

KEY

- MORE THAN 1,300
- 650-1,300
- 260-650
- 130-260
- 65-130
- 5-65
- LESS THAN 5
- 0

LEFT This map shows how many people live per square mile around the world.

Is the world's population spread evenly?

No. Most parts of the world are empty of people, while others, such as Tokyo, in Japan, are very overcrowded. Today most people in North America, Europe, and Australia live in towns and cities. In other parts of the world the majority of people live in the countryside. Cities are constantly growing as people move into them to find work.

Do some people live up mountains?

People live in the mountains in many parts of the world. They have to travel over steep roads to get anywhere and cope with harsh weather in winter. Humans have found ways of living in all kinds of places. They learned to farm steep land by building terraces (left).

ABOVE This village in Cambodia is built on stilts above a river.

Are homes different around the world?

Yes! Some house styles look similar, but in many places houses have to be built to suit the weather, the land, or the number of people. People who live in places that sometimes flood build their houses on stilts, or wooden legs, to raise them above the water. On mountains, people build houses with sloping roofs so the snow will slide off.

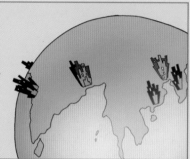

DID YOU KNOW?
A megacity is a city with more than 10 million inhabitants. Today, there are about 20 megacities around the world.

What is a nomad?

A nomad is a person who does not settle in one place. In parts of Asia, some nomads travel around in search of fresh places for their animals to graze. In Africa, they may travel to find new water sources. In European countries, some groups of Roma (gypsies) and other traveling people live in caravans or mobile homes and travel from place to place.

RIGHT A yurt is a type of portable home used by the nomad people of Mongolia.

GOVERNMENTS

Where are governments based?

Governments are based in their country's capital city. Government representatives from the rest of the country meet together in offices in the capital to make decisions and discuss matters, such as new laws. Because the capital city is an important place, other business and financial institutions set up there, too. Many capital cities become extremely large. Mexico City, for example, is home to about 20 million people.

ABOVE The Capitol Building in Washington, D.C., is home to the United States government.

Why do people vote?

People vote in elections to choose people to lead them, for example, in a government. In what is called a democracy, voters have a choice of leaders. When chosen, the leaders work for the people. The opposite of a democracy is a dictatorship. Dictatorships do not allow people to choose their leader and one person may control the whole country.

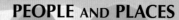

RIGHT Governments make decisions after a debate like this one, in the House of Commons, United Kingdom.

What do governments do?

Governments run countries. They make laws and defend their country using armed forces. They are responsible for public services, such as schools and hospitals. Governments raise money to do these things by charging people taxes. A government is usually led by a president or prime minister.

Do kings and queens still rule countries?

There are still a small number of countries in the world, such as Saudi Arabia, that are personally ruled by a king. Today, most of the world's remaining kingdoms are democracies where the king or queen is the head of the country, but daily government is carried out by people elected by voters. There are at least 50 kings and queens in the world. They inherit their title when a previous king or queen dies or retires.

LEFT King Carl Gustav and Queen Silvia are the king and queen of Sweden, a country ruled by a democratic government.

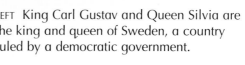

67

THE WORLD OF WORK

ABOVE A giant combine harvester cuts the wheat fields on the vast plains of the American Midwest.

Where are the biggest farms?

The biggest farms in the world are in the United States and Canada. In the United States, for example, farmers grow immense fields of crops, such as wheat. To grow such large amounts of food, these farms rely on modern machines and chemical sprays that get rid of weeds and insect pests. This type of farming is called intensive farming.

What is the world's biggest fishing net?

Some giant fishing boats have nets that stretch as wide as a football field! These are dragged through the ocean to scoop up fish. Fishing is an important industry for many people around the world. There are about 3 million people working in fishing boats in the sea. They catch so many fish that in some parts of the oceans fish have become scarce.

Where is the world's busiest factory?

Many people say that China is like the world's busiest and biggest factory. A factory is a place that makes many copies of the same thing to sell. Vast amounts of the goods the world buys come from China, including clothing, watches, and cell phones. Over half of the world's cameras and a third of the world's televisions are made in China.

LEFT The Eiffel Tower in Paris, France, brings in much money from tourism.

Is tourism important?

Tourism is an important industry all over the world because it creates many jobs, for example, in hotels and restaurants. It also brings in money from foreign visitors. The most visited destination in the world for foreign tourists is Paris, in France. People come here to enjoy the famous museums, palaces, and the Eiffel Tower.

DID YOU KNOW?

Some cattle and sheep farms in Australia are so big farmers use planes instead of tractors to check on their animals.

RICH AND POOR

Why are some countries richer than others?

There are many reasons why some countries are richer than others. One reason is that they have "natural resources." These can be valuable things, such as oil, coal, trees, or diamonds. People can dig up or harvest these resources and sell them, or make them into goods they can sell. But it is important to remember that even in rich countries there are still poor people.

RIGHT This oil refinery produces valuable barrels of oil that a country can sell.

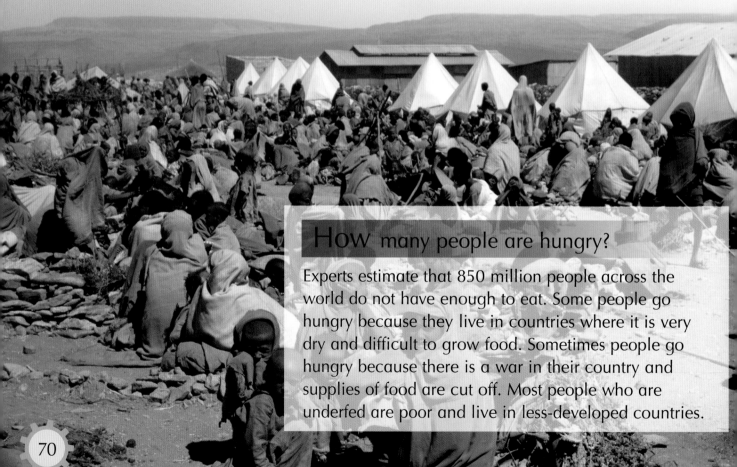

How many people are hungry?

Experts estimate that 850 million people across the world do not have enough to eat. Some people go hungry because they live in countries where it is very dry and difficult to grow food. Sometimes people go hungry because there is a war in their country and supplies of food are cut off. Most people who are underfed are poor and live in less-developed countries.

What are shanty towns?

Shanty towns are groups of homes built from scrap materials, such as pieces of wood and sheets of metal or plastic. They are often found on the edge of cities. Shanty towns are made by people who came to find work but who remain poor. These towns often have no running water. Fires sometimes break out because most people here use fire for cooking and warmth.

Who helps people in need?

Groups of people working for charities raise money to help people in need. Most try to provide the means for people to rebuild their own lives. For example, they might give farmers tools or seeds, or provide training for someone to learn a new skill. They also help educate children in less-developed countries so they can get a job when they grow up.

KEEPING IN TOUCH

When do we communicate?

Communication happens when we pass signals to each other. It is something we do every day. We communicate through speech and through written words, through hand gestures, and with the expressions on our faces. People with limited hearing use a special form of communication by making hand signs. They can also read the shape of our lips when we speak.

How many different languages are there?

There may be as many as 8,000 in the world. In many countries, people may speak the national language and also a local dialect (form of speech). The most common language in the world is Chinese (Mandarin). Outside China the most widely spoken language is English.

RIGHT Some of these signs in Ireland are written in English and also in the old language of Ireland, Gaelic.

Who reads from right to left?

People who read books in Arabic or Hebrew read from right to left. Some languages, such as Japanese, are written from the top of the page to the bottom. Different languages often have different alphabets. The English alphabet has 26 letters but the alphabet used in Cambodia has 74!

LEFT Many people in China and Japan practice calligraphy—the art of writing words beautifully.

DID YOU KNOW?
Esperanto is a special language that does not belong to one country but was invented over 100 years ago as an international language.

How do phone calls travel across the world?

Communications satellites in space pick up telephone signals and transfer them to receivers on the other side of the world. Today we can communicate instantly with people far away. The satellites are also used for Internet connections so that people all over the world can keep in touch using e-mail.

Satellite

Receiver

FESTIVALS AND SPECIAL DAYS

What happens at Jewish Passover?

Passover is an important religious festival that Jews celebrate with special prayers and food. It begins with the Seder—a meal and a story about the history of Passover. Passover is the time the Jews were led out of slavery in Egypt by the prophet Moses. The festival lasts for eight days.

When is Chinese New Year?

Chinese New Year is in February. Before the New Year celebrations begin, people clean their homes to chase away evil spirits. During the celebrations, people share special meals, give each other gifts, and set off fireworks. There are also dances with large dragon and lion costumes. The dragon, a symbol of strength, is thought to repel evil and bring good luck.

RIGHT These girls are decorating Easter eggs with colored paints. People eat chocolate eggs at Easter because eggs represent new life. Easter Sunday commemorates the day Jesus Christ came to life again. It is the most important festival in the Christian calendar.

DID YOU KNOW?
Although Myanmar (Burma) in South Asia is usually dry and hot in April, it is always wet at the New Year celebrations, called Thingyan, because people spray each other with water!

What is a carnival?

In ancient Rome, there was a rowdy winter festival called *saturnalia*. People copied this idea in the Middle Ages. They feasted before Lent began, when Christians had to give up eating meat. People still celebrate carnival today. In New Orleans, jazz bands parade.

What is the festival of light?

The festival of light, called Diwali, celebrates the coming of the Hindu New Year in October or November. Diwali lasts over five days. Stories told during this time celebrate the victory of good over evil and knowledge over ignorance. People decorate buildings with candles and colored lights, and they make delicious treats.

75

ART AND MUSIC

Do dances tell stories?

Yes, many dances in different cultures across the world are used to tell stories. In India, kathakali dances tell stories of gods and demons. And some ballets, such as *The Nutcracker*, use graceful movements to tell a fairy tale. Other types of dances are used to express a mood or a feeling or are just for fun. Certain dances are only performed at celebrations, such as weddings.

RIGHT Kathakali dancing is a spectacular combination of drama, dance, music, and ritual.

What is street theater?

Street theater is when people perform plays in outdoor public places, such as shopping centers. In a real theater there are lights and plenty of space for props and costumes. In street theater actors have very simple props and often have to shout to be heard. People buy a ticket to go into a theater, but usually pay street performers what they think a show is worth after it is over.

Where do dreamtime paintings come from?

Dreamtime paintings are made by the Aboriginal peoples of Australia. These artists use many dots to form symbols and shapes that describe a time in the past before there were people, when spirit gods created the rivers, rocks, and mountains. Like many types of painting, these images are powerful because they tell stories without using words.

DID YOU KNOW?
The oldest musical instrument of all is the human voice! People have always sung songs. Sometimes people sing together in choirs of hundreds of singers.

LEFT Steel drum music began in Trinidad and Tobago in the 1940s. It is influenced by African drum music.

What is "world music"?

"World music" is music that has an international appeal but is the traditional sound of one particular country. Sometimes the traditional music of a country is connected to a certain instrument. In Indonesia, for example, gamelan musicians play music on bronze xylophones. In Spain, flamenco is played on guitars and dancers accompany the music. In Jamica, steel drum bands make a rich sound.

CHILDREN AROUND THE WORLD

What games do children play?

Around the world, children play a great variety of games. Some, such as marbles, soccer, and other ball games, are played in nearly every country. In some countries, children play with expensive toys or computer games. In other countries, such as South Africa, some children make their own toys from recycled pieces of wire and cans.

RIGHT This American boy is practicing his baseball pitch. Baseball is a national sport in the United States.

Why do some children work?

Some children work to help their parents. They may help with farm chores before they go to school. Some children work all day instead of going to school. This is often because their parents are poor and need help to earn money. In many countries, this is illegal and young people may only work part-time.

When do children start school?

The age at which children start elementary school varies between countries. In India, children start school at the age of five. In Norway and Russia, children start at seven. In elementary school, children learn to read and write, although for some children this may be in a different language from the one they speak at home.

BELOW In an elementary school, children may learn all their subjects from a single teacher.

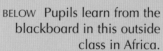

DID YOU KNOW?
The legal age at which a child becomes an adult varies between countries. In Iran it is 15, in the United States and most of Europe it is 18, while in some parts of Africa it is 13!

BELOW Pupils learn from the blackboard in this outside class in Africa.

Where do children learn outside?

In some of the world's poorer countries, classes take place outside because there are few school buildings. In parts of Nepal, some people live in remote areas, and children walk several miles to school and back each day. Some schools may have fewer classes because they may be short of books, tables, pens, and pencils.

CLOTHES THAT PEOPLE WEAR

What is national dress?

National dress is the clothing traditionally worn by people in a particular country. Around the world today many people wear similar sorts of clothes, but some people still wear traditional dress every day or on special occasions, such as festivals, weddings, or religious celebrations. Traditional dress does not change with fashion.

LEFT This Japanese girl is wearing a traditional kimono (gown) tied with an obi (sash).

Who wears saris?

In many hot countries, people wear long loose clothes to keep out the heat of the sun. These clothes are sometimes white or light-colored because light colors reflect instead of absorb heat, and this helps to keep people cool. It is also important to choose natural fabrics, such as cotton or linen, because these fabrics are cool and better at absorbing perspiration.

Where do soldiers wear skirts?

Guards of honor in the Greek army are called Evzónes. Their uniform is based on the old-fashion costume of the mountain peoples—a white skirt, woolen tights, and a cap with a tassel.

LEFT These firefighters wear distinctive orange clothes that also protect them.

DID YOU KNOW?
On a cold day, about 70 percent of your total body heat is lost through your head. That is why it is important to wear a hat in the winter.

RIGHT This Sikh woman is wearing a traditional red wedding dress.

Why are some colors special?

The color of a piece of clothing can be special when it is worn for particular ceremonies or reasons. For example, black is the traditional color of mourning and is worn as a mark of respect at funerals in western countries. In China and India, people wear white for funerals and in parts of Africa they wear red. And while white is the traditional color for wedding dresses in western countries, in China it is red.

THE FOOD WE EAT

What are staple foods?

Staple foods are filling foods that provide energy. They are usually carbohydrates, such as rice. The staples people eat are those that grow well in their local area. Corn is a staple in Central America and potatoes are staples in North America and Europe.

Where do pineapples grow?

Pineapples and other tropical fruit, such as bananas and mangoes, grow best in countries where it is warm all year. Different crops need different climates and soils. That is why some foods are more common in some places than others. For example, apples grow better in temperate, or milder, climates.

DID YOU KNOW?
About half the world's people eat insects as part of their diet. In total, about 1,500 different species of insect are eaten by people in various parts of the world.

LEFT These farmers carry pineapples on a special rack that does not bruise the fruit.

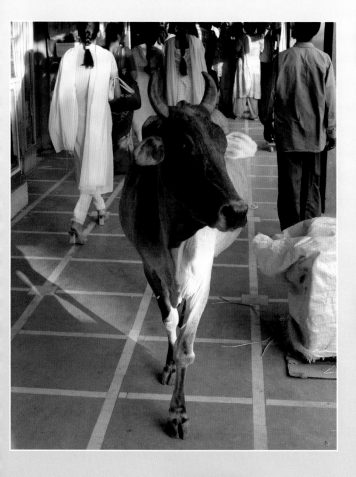

Who doesn't eat meat?

Vegetarians are people who do not eat meat. People of certain religions also have rules about what foods they eat. Hindus do not eat beef because for them the cow is a holy animal (left). Muslims and Jews do not eat pork because it is considered an unclean animal. Traditionally, Catholics do not eat red meat on Friday and this is why fish is a popular dinner at the end of the week.

Who eats with chopsticks?

People in Southeast Asian countries, such as China, eat with chopsticks—as do people in many other parts of the world when they eat Southeast Asian food. Chopsticks are held between the thumb and index finger. In the West, most people eat with knives, forks, and spoons. In India, many people eat with their fingers.

BELOW Picking up slippery noodles with chopsticks takes some practice!

COUNTRY CONNECTIONS

HOW are countries connected?

One of the ways in which countries are connected is through trade. For example, bananas only grow in tropical regions. People in Europe and North America like to eat bananas and depend upon the banana farmers to grow the fruit. The farmers rely upon the countries that buy the fruit because this trade pays their wages. This is called being interdependent.

WHICH is the world's longest road?

The Pan-American Highway. It covers 30,000 miles, from Alaska right down to Central America. There is still a section missing in the middle, but the road starts up again and carries on through South America to Chile, Argentina and Brazil.

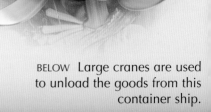

BELOW Large cranes are used to unload the goods from this container ship.

What is fair trade?

Fair trade is when the people who grow or make products for export get paid a fair price. Fair trade companies make sure that workers are treated fairly and are not made to work in dangerous conditions or for long hours. Many fair trade products have special labels so that shoppers can choose to support these standards of fairness.

RIGHT An East Asian fair trade farmer harvests a rice crop.

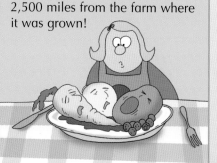

DID YOU KNOW?
Many of us eat food that that has traveled between 1,500 and 2,500 miles from the farm where it was grown!

Are people the same across the world?

People everywhere are connected because we all share the same basic needs. People who live in the same country may be defined by their nationality, such as Indian or Chinese, but today many different peoples live in one country and many countries are "multicultural."

Plants

Growing in the sun ➤

GREEN LEAVES

Plants reduce carbon dioxide and produce vital oxygen through photosynthesis.

There are 287,655 named species of plants, although many more are believed to exist. These range from trees, bushes, and herbs to grasses, ferns, and mosses. Most plants get their energy for growing from sunlight, using a process called photosynthesis.

➤ HOW DO GREEN PLANTS FEED?

Green plants make their own food in a process called photosynthesis. Chlorophyll helps to trap energy from the sun. Plants use this energy to convert water and carbon dioxide into sugars and starch.

➤ WHY ARE MOST PLANTS GREEN?

Most plants are green because they contain the green pigment chlorophyll in their stems and leaves. Sometimes the green pigment is masked by other colors, such as red. This means that not all plants that contain chlorophyll look green.

❯ HOW DOES A FLOWER FORM SO QUICKLY?

When a flower opens out from a bud, it may appear in just a few hours. This is possible because the flower is already formed in miniature inside the bud, just waiting to open out. The bud opens as its cells take in water and grow.

BLOSSOMING

Buds open in the warm and sunny weather of spring.

❯ HOW MUCH SUGAR DOES PHOTOSYNTHESIS MAKE IN A YEAR?

Plants turn the sugar they make by photosynthesis into other chemical compounds that they need for growth and development. They also use sugar to make energy. Some scientists have estimated that the total mass of green plants alive in the entire world makes more than 190 billion tons of sugar every year by photosynthesis.

❯ WHAT MAKES A SEED GROW?

To grow, a seed needs moisture, warmth, and air. Some seeds can only germinate (begin to grow) if they have first been in the low temperatures of winter. The seeds of some plants can lie dormant (inactive) for years before germinating.

WHY DO SHOOTS GROW UPWARD?

Most shoots grow upward, toward the sunlight. The growing tip of the shoot can detect the direction of the light, and chemicals are released that make it grow more on the lower or darker side, thus turning the shoot upward.

SHOOTING UP

Like most plants, a bean shoot relies on the soil for water and support.

Feeding

Plants need water, mineral salts, and foods, such as carbohydrates, in order to grow. Green plants make their own foods, while other plants may take in food from de-caying plants or animals, or directly from other living plants.

❯ HOW DOES A PARASITIC PLANT FEED?

Parasitic plants do not need to make their own food, and many are not green. Instead, they grow into the tissues of another plant, called the host, and tap into its food and water transportation system, taking all the nourishment they need.

ROOTS

Roots anchor the plant while taking in water and mineral salts.

❯ HOW DOES A VENUS FLYTRAP CATCH ITS PREY?

The flytrap is a carnivorous (meat-eating) plant that catches insects and other small animals. The trap is a flattened, hinged pad at the end of each leaf, fringed with bristles. When an insect lands on the pad and touches one of the sensitive hairs growing there, the trap is sprung and closes over the insect.

TOP ? QUESTION

WHY DO ROOTS GROW DOWNWARD?

Roots grow down because the root responds to gravity by releasing chemicals that prevent growth on the lower side, thus turning the root downward.

❯ HOW DOES MISTLETOE FEED?

Mistletoe is a hemi-parasitic plant, which means that it takes some of its nutrients from a host plant and some from its own photosynthesis. It can attach itself to the branches of many different trees and shrubs.

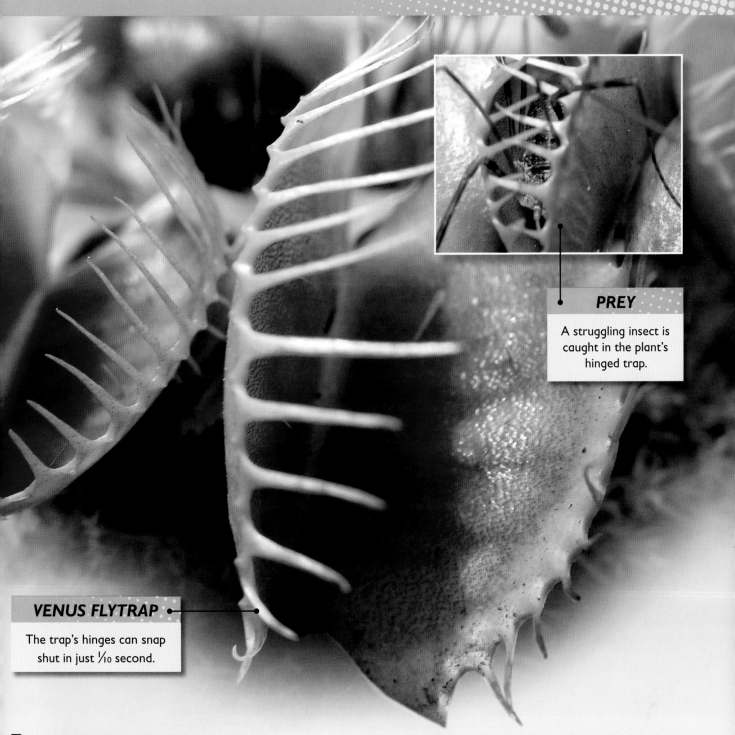

PREY

A struggling insect is caught in the plant's hinged trap.

VENUS FLYTRAP

The trap's hinges can snap shut in just 1/10 second.

➤ HOW DO PLANTS TAKE IN WATER?

Plants use their extensive root systems to take in water from the ground. Each root branches into a network of rootlets, which in turn bear root hairs. Water passes into the root across the cell walls of millions of tiny root hairs.

➤ HOW FAST DOES SAP FLOW THROUGH A TREE?

Sap is the fluid that transports water and food through plants. Sap may flow through a tree as fast as 3 feet every hour.

Reproduction

Many plants reproduce by pollination. The pollen, containing the male cells, fertilizes the female ovules, which then produce seeds. The pollen can be taken to its destination by insects, birds, the wind, or water.

› WHAT HAPPENS IN A FLOWER AFTER POLLINATION?

After pollination, the pollen that has landed on the stigma of another flower of the same species will begin to germinate if conditions are right. It sends a tube down into the ovary of the flower, which it enters to fertilize an ovule. Each ovule can now become a seed.

› WHICH FLOWERS LAST FOR JUST ONE DAY?

The flowers of morning glory and daylilies open each morning and shrivel and die toward evening.

MORNING GLORY

The flowers are pollinated by bees, hummingbirds, butterflies, and moths.

› CAN PLANTS REPRODUCE WITHOUT SEEDS?

Some plants, such as mosses, liverworts, and ferns, do not produce seeds. Instead, they spread by dispersing spores, which can produce a new plant without the need of pollination. Other plants can reproduce by growing runners or splitting off from bulbs, or swollen stems.

HOW ARE FLOWERS POLLINATED?

Many flowers have evolved their colors and scent to attract insects. The animal lands on the flower, gets showered with pollen, then moves to the next flower, transporting the pollen.

• *SOWING SEEDS*

Seeds must be dispersed, or spread around, so that some will find suitable places to germinate. Seeds contained in berries and fruit are spread in bird droppings.

POLLINATION

Bees, wasps, and butterflies like to feed from flowers' nectar.

❯ WHICH FLOWERS ARE POLLINATED BY MAMMALS?

The flowers of the African baobab tree are pollinated by bushbabies and bats.

❯ HOW ARE SEEDS DISPERSED?

Many seeds are dispersed by animals. Birds eat berries and pass out the tougher seeds unharmed in their droppings. Some fruit capsules have hooks that catch in animal fur and are transported that way. Many seeds can be carried by the wind. The sycamore has "helicopter" wings to carry it along.

Plants and the environment >

Plants are vital to the environment. In fact, without plants, there would be no life on our planet. Plants are key producers of oxygen, which most animals need to survive. Many animals, including humans, rely on plants for shelter, water, food, and oxygen.

CATERPILLAR
A tree's leaves may provide food for caterpillars.

> WHAT IS THE NITROGEN CYCLE?

Bacteria in the soil use nitrogen from the air and turn it into a form that plants can use. Plants then use the nitrogen in their cells to make complex compounds, such as proteins. When animals eat plants, the nitrogen returns to the soil in their droppings. It also returns when plant and animal bodies decay and rot.

> HOW DO PLANTS RECYCLE WATER?

Plants help to return water to the air through the process of transpiration. This is when water evaporates from the stems and leaves of plants. Water enters the plant through its roots. A column of water moves up through the plant, from the roots all the way through the trunk or stem, into the leaves.

TOP QUESTION

WHAT LIVES IN A TREE?

Many species of beetles lay their eggs in a tree's bark. Birds select a fork in a branch to build a nest, or use a natural hole in the trunk, and wild bees may also choose to nest inside a hollow tree. Many mammals are tree dwellers, including squirrels, monkeys, sloths, bats, and koalas.

➤ HOW ARE PLANTS USED TO CLEAN UP SEWAGE?

Sewage treatment plants use tiny algae and other microscopic organisms in their filter beds. These algae and other organisms feed on the pollutants in the water and help to make it clean.

HERBIVORE

Caterpillars are the larvae of moths and butterflies. They only eat plant matter.

➤ HOW DO FORESTS HELP IMPROVE THE AIR?

Forests do this by releasing huge quantities of water vapor and oxygen into the atmosphere. Plants also absorb carbon dioxide, and help prevent this gas from building up to damaging levels.

95

Plants and the soil >

Plants take water and nutrients from the soil, only to return them in a never-ending, finely balanced cycle. But this cycle can be destroyed by humans if we forget to care for our vital forests and fields.

> WHAT HAPPENS TO ALL THE LEAVES THAT FALL?

Huge quantities of leaves fall from forest trees, but they do not build up on the woodland floor from year to year. The dead leaves are attacked, for example by fungi and bacteria, and break down, becoming part of the soil. The leaves are also eaten by animals, including worms and insects.

> HOW DO PLANTS MAKE SOIL MORE FERTILE?

When plants die, they decompose, releasing the chemicals in their tissues into the surrounding soil. The mixture of rotting leaves and other plant material in the soil is called humus, and this makes the soil more fertile.

LEAF FOOD

Fallen leaves provide food for animals and fertilize the soil.

❯ WHAT IS OVERGRAZING?

It is when livestock, such as cows and sheep, are allowed to eat the grasses and other plants in one area for too long. The plants are not able to recover and, in dry areas, the land may become eroded or turn into desert.

❯ HOW DO PLANTS COLONIZE BARE GROUND?

Some plants can quickly colonize bare soil by germinating rapidly from lightweight, wind-blown seeds. Some colonizing plants spread by growing runners, which split off, becoming new plants.

HOW DO PLANTS HELP US RECLAIM LAND?

Several types of grass, including marram, can be planted on coastal dunes. Their roots anchor the sand and help to stop it from blowing away. Plants can even begin to reclaim land contaminated by industrial poisons. Some species have evolved forms that can tolerate toxic substances. They gradually improve the fertility and build up the soil so that other plants can grow there, too.

DANDELION

A dandelion's seeds are carried by "parachutes" to take root on bare ground.

❯ HOW CAN PLANTS BE USED TO HELP STOP EROSION?

Erosion is when soil is loosened and removed by the action of natural force, such as wind and water. This can often be reduced or prevented by using plants. The roots of the plants trap the loose soil and stop it from being blown away. This can be useful on steep slopes or the edges of deserts.

Plants as food →

About 12,000 species of plants are known to have been used as food by people, and about 150 of these are in regular cultivation. Human cultivation of plants is part of agriculture, along with raising animals. Without agriculture, there would be no human civilization.

› WHAT ARE THE MOST IMPORTANT FOOD CROPS?

The most important crops are the cereals, such as wheat, rice, and corn (maize). These form the basis of many people's diet. Tuber crops, such as potatoes, are also widely grown. All these foods provide carbohydrates, while legumes, such as peas, beans, and lentils, are rich in protein.

PEACHES

Peaches grow well in warm climates such as the Mediterranean and the southern United States.

› WHICH FRUITS ARE GROWN FOR FOOD?

Fruits of the temperate regions include apples, pears, and strawberries. In warmer regions, there are citrus fruits, such as oranges and lemons, and other fruits, such as papayas, pineapples, and melons. Some fruits have a savory flavor, such as avocados and bell peppers.

SUGAR MAPLE

Maple syrup is often used as a sweetener with pancakes.

➤ WHAT TREES GIVE US A SWEET, SUGARY SYRUP?

The sugar maple has a sweet sap, which is harvested to make maple syrup. Most maple syrup comes from the province of Quebec, in Canada.

➤ WHAT IS THE AMAZON COW-TREE?

The Amazon cow-tree is a tropical fig. It takes its name from the fact that it produces a milk-like sap, or latex, which can be drunk just like cow's milk.

SUNFLOWER

Sunflower oil is commonly used for frying food and contains essential vitamin E.

➤ WHICH PLANTS GIVE US OIL?

The seeds of many plants are rich in oil, which they store as a source of food and energy. We extract oil from several of these plants, including olives, sunflowers, corn (maize), soy beans, peanuts, rapeseed, sesame, and African oil palm.

➤ WHAT PLANTS ARE USED TO MAKE SUGAR?

The main source of sugar is the sweet stems of sugar cane, a tall grass that grows in tropical countries. In some temperate areas, including Europe, there are large crops of sugar beet. This plant stores sugar in its thickened roots. In some parts of the tropics, the sap of the sugar palm is made into sugar.

Harvesting the land →

It is not just our staple crops, such as cereals and potatoes, that are provided by plants. Drinks, such as tea, coffee, wine, and beer, are made from plants. Sometimes we do not even notice the plants on our plate, such as the pectin from plant cells that stiffens gelatin.

› WHAT IS BREADFRUIT?

Breadfruit is a tree native to the Malay Archipelego. It grows to about 65 feet and has large edible fruit, which is eaten as a vegetable. The related jackfruit, from India and Malaysia, also has edible fruits up to 24 inches long.

EAR OF WHEAT

Wheat is used to make flour for bread, cookies, cakes, pasta, noodles, and couscous.

› WHERE DID WHEAT COME FROM?

Wheat is one of the oldest known crops. It was probably first cultivated over 6,000 years ago in Mesopotamia (present-day Iraq). Many useful crop plants have their origins in the Middle East. Other examples are barley, oats and rye, peas and lentils, onions, olives, figs, apples, and pears.

TOP QUESTION ?

HOW IS TEA MADE?

Tea comes from the leaves of a camellia grown on hillsides in India, Sri Lanka, Indonesia, Japan, and China. The young leaf tips are harvested, dried, and then crushed to make tea.

TEA PICKING

After water, tea is the world's most consumed drink.

❯ HOW IS CHOCOLATE MADE?

The cacao tree comes originally from the lowland rain forests of the Amazon and Orinoco. The fruit, called pods, develops on the sides of the trunk, and each pod contains about 20 to 60 seeds—the cocoa "beans." The beans must be fermented, roasted, and ground before they become cocoa powder, the raw material for making chocolate.

❯ WHERE DOES COFFEE COME FROM?

The coffee plant is a large shrub, and its berries are used to make coffee. The ripe berries are harvested, then dried to remove the flesh from the hard pits inside. These are the coffee "beans," which are then often roasted.

❯ WHERE WERE POTATOES FIRST GROWN?

Potatoes grow wild in the Andes Mountains of South America and were first gathered as food by the native people of that region. All the many varieties grown today derive from that wild source.

COCOA POD

Today, cocoa is a highly valuable crop in west Africa and the Caribbean.

Plants as medicine →

ROSY PERIWINKLE

Extracts from this plant, vinblastine and vincristine, are used by many international drug companies.

Plants have been used as medicine for at least 100,000 years. In much of the world, especially in China and India, herbal remedies are used more than any other kind of medicine. Today, scientists are still researching the valuable healing properties of plants for use in conventional medicines.

❯ CAN PLANTS HELP FIGHT CANCER?

Several plants are effective against cancer tumors. One of the most famous is the rosy periwinkle. One of its extracts, vincristine, is very effective against some types of leukemia, a cancer of the blood.

❯ WHICH PLANTS AID DIGESTION?

Many plants, including the herbs and spices used in cooking, help digestion. In Europe, the bitter extract of wild gentians provides a good remedy for digestive problems.

➤ WHAT IS GINSENG?

Ginseng is a plant related to ivy, and has been used in herbal medicine for centuries. It is claimed—but not proved—to help many conditions, including fatigue and depression, kidney disease, heart problems, and headaches.

➤ WHICH PLANT HELPS COMBAT MALARIA?

Quinine, from the bark of the quinine tree, which grows in the South American Andes, can cure or prevent malaria. Before the widespread use of quinine, malaria used to kill 2 million people each year.

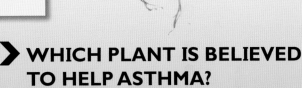

GINSENG

Ginseng root is often taken in dried form.

➤ WHICH PLANT IS BELIEVED TO HELP ASTHMA?

Lungwort is a herb with purple flowers and spotted leaves that are said to look like lungs. For this reason, it is sometimes used to treat asthma. There is no definite proof that it works.

LUNGWORT

The lungwort herb gets its name from the belief that it helps the lungs.

➤ CAN WILLOWS HELP PAIN?

Willow twigs were once chewed to give pain relief. A compound similar to the drug aspirin was once extracted from willows and the herb meadowsweet, known as spiraea—giving aspirin its name.

Materials from plants >

Plant materials are an essential part of our lives, keeping us warm, dry, safe, and even—in the case of musical instruments—entertained. From wood to leaves, plants supply many of our raw materials.

> WHAT TYPES OF THINGS CAN BE MADE FROM PLANTS?

We make all kinds of things from plant materials. Wood alone is used to make countless objects, big and small, from construction lumber to toys. All kinds of cloth are also made from plants—and so is the paper you are looking at!

HOW MANY THINGS CAN BE MADE FROM BAMBOO?

Bamboo is one of the world's most useful plant products. It is used for scaffolding and building houses, and for making paper, furniture, pipes, canes, and (when split) for mats, hats, umbrellas, baskets, blinds, fans, and brushes. Some bamboos have young shoots that are delicious to eat.

> WHAT IS JOJOBA?

Jojoba is a bush found in Mexico. The fruits have a high-grade oily wax. It is used as a lubricant, in printing inks, and in body lotions and shampoo.

> WHAT ARE VIOLINS MADE OF?

The body of a violin is usually made from finely carved spruce and maple woods, creating its beautiful sound.

THATCHED COTTAGE

Traditional English cottages have a wood frame and roofs of thatched straw.

➤ WHAT IS BALSA?

Balsa is the world's lightest wood—it floats high in water. Balsa trees grow in tropical South America. Balsa wood is used for making models, such as airplanes, and also for rafts, life preservers, and insulation.

➤ WHAT IS RAFFIA?

Raffia is a natural fiber made from the young leaves of the raffia palm, which grows in tropical Africa. Raffia is used in handicrafts, such as basketry.

RAFFIA BAGS

Dyeing and weaving raffia is a traditional handicraft.

BAMBOO CAFÉ

Giant bamboo plants shade bamboo furniture in China.

Plant products

Plant products are chosen for different uses, depending on their natural properties. The softness of cotton makes it ideal for clothing. The springiness of rubber makes it perfect for products from rubber bands to rubber gloves.

> WHAT IS KAPOK?

Kapok is similar to cotton. It comes from the kapok tree, which is cultivated in Asia and can be as tall as 160 feet. The fluffy seed fibers are used to stuff mattresses, jackets, quilts, and sleeping bags.

> HOW IS CORK PRODUCED?

Cork comes from a tree called the cork oak. The cork is the thick, spongy bark. It is stripped away from the lower trunk, then left to grow back for up to 10 years before the next harvest. Cork is used to make many things, from bottle corks and bulletin boards to floor tiles.

CORK OAK

Cork oaks grow wild around the Mediterranean Sea and have been cultivated in Portugal and Spain.

COTTON

Cotton plants grow in the Americas, India, and Africa.

❯ HOW IS COTTON TURNED INTO CLOTH?

Cotton is a soft fiber that grows naturally around the seeds of the cotton plant, forming "bolls." These are "ginned" to remove the seeds; spun, or twisted, into thread; and then woven to make cloth.

❯ WHAT IS RUBBER?

Rubber is the sap of some plants, particularly the para rubber tree. The trees are pierced, or tapped, and the sap drips slowly into a waiting container.

❯ WHAT WOOD MAKES THE BEST CRICKET BAT?

The best bats are made in India, from the wood of the cricket bat willow, a white willow. The blade (the part the ball strikes) is made from willow, and the handle from a different wood or cane.

WILLOW BAT

Willow is lightweight but will not splinter when hit by a ball.

❯ CAN PLANTS PRODUCE FUEL TO RUN CARS?

The copaiba tree of the Amazon rain forest yields an oil similar to diesel fuel that can be used to run engines. Oilseed rape, soybean, and the petroleum nut tree of Southeast Asia can also be used to produce biofuels, or plant fuels. As crude oil reserves are used up, biofuels may become more important.

Extreme plants

The many species of plants are all competing for resources. They have evolved countless extreme survival strategies, from great height to immense roots. They have adapted to hostile environments, from deserts to mountains, so that they can find a place to grow and thrive.

WHICH IS THE LARGEST SEED?

The coco de mer of the Seychelles has the largest seeds, each weighing up to 48 pounds. They are produced inside a big fruit that takes six years to grow.

WHAT IS THE SMALLEST FLOWERING PLANT?

A tiny tropical floating duckweed is the world's smallest flowering plant. Some species measure less than one-fiftieth of an inch across, even when full grown.

DUCKWEED

These simple plants just consist of a platelike structure that floats on the water surface.

BANYAN TREE

This single banyan looks as if it is a whole grove of trees.

WHAT IS THE OLDEST PLANT?

The oldest known plant may be the creosote bush. It grows in the southwestern United States and in Mexico. Some of these bushes are thought to be 11,700 years old. The bristlecone pine, which grows mainly in the southwestern United States, notably in the White Mountains of California, is also extremely old. The oldest is about 4,900 years old.

➤ WHAT PLANT CAN SPREAD ACROSS THE WIDEST AREA?

The banyan of India and Pakistan often starts life as an epiphyte—a small plant growing on another tree. As it grows, it sends down woody roots that come to resemble tree trunks. Eventually it can seem like a grove of separate trees. One 200-year-old banyan had 100 "trunks."

OLD PINE

Although the original branches die, bristlecone pines can live for 5,000 years.

➤ WHICH PLANT HAS THE LONGEST LEAF?

The raffia palm of tropical Africa produces the longest known leaves. The stalk can be nearly 13 feet and the leaf blade over 65 feet long.

➤ HOW DEEP ARE THE DEEPEST ROOTS?

Roots of a South African fig were found to have penetrated 400 feet below the dry surface.

Plant records >

Tall conifers tower above other plants in their forest, while giant flowers feed among roots on the ground. In the oceans and lakes, seaweeds and waterlilies grow huge to absorb nutrients and sunlight.

WHAT IS THE LARGEST FLOWER?

It's the rafflesia, which grows in Southeast Asia. It is a parasite, growing on the stems of lianas in the forest. Flowers can measure 35 inches—and they stink, mimicking the aroma of rotting flesh to attract flies to pollinate the flower.

› WHICH PLANT GROWS THE SLOWEST?

The record for the slowest-growing plant probably goes to the dioon plant. The dioon grows in Mexico, and one specimen was recorded to have an average growth rate of one thirty-fifth of an inch per year.

› WHICH PLANT GROWS THE FASTEST?

The giant bamboo of Burma grows at up to 1 foot per day, making it one of the fastest growing of all plants. However, another species from India, the spiny bamboo, holds the record for growth in a greenhouse—it achieved 35 inches in a day.

> WHAT IS THE WORLD'S LONGEST SEAWEED?

Giant kelp is a huge seaweed that forms underwater forests in the coastal waters of California. Its fronds can be over 200 feet long, making it one of the tallest plants known.

GIANT KELP

Kelp forests are vital ecosystems that are home to many animals, from fish and starfish to sea urchins.

> WHICH IS THE TALLEST TREE?

The California redwood, which grows along the North American Pacific coast, is the tallest tree in the world, reaching 368 feet. Some Australian eucalyptus trees can grow to 300 feet.

> WHICH PLANT HAS THE LARGEST FLOATING LEAVES?

The giant water lily of the Amazon region has huge leaves. They grow up to almost 9 feet across, and can support the weight of a child.

GIANT WATER LILY

These lilies, which grow in still lakes and swamps, have stalks up to 23 feet long.

Life on the land

Rodents

Rodents are mammals, which means they have backbones, they are hairy, and they produce milk to feed their young. Rodents are distinguished by having continuously growing incisor teeth. Squirrels, hamsters, beavers, rats, and mice are all rodents.

WHY DO RODENTS HAVE LONG TEETH?

The two sharp teeth, called incisors, at the front of the rodent's jaw are the ones it uses for gnawing. A rodent's incisors get worn down as it gnaws tough food, but they keep on growing throughout its life.

NUTRIA TEETH

The nutria, which lives in wetlands, has huge, orange incisor teeth.

TOP QUESTION ?

WHY DO BEAVERS BUILD DAMS?

Beavers build their lodges, or homes, in streams or rivers. But first they need to build a dam to make an area of still water, or the current would wash the lodge away. With their huge front teeth, the beavers cut down trees to build the dam. They plaster the sides with mud and fill gaps with stones and sticks.

› WHICH IS THE BIGGEST RODENT?

The largest rodent in the world is the capybara, which lives in South America. It measures up to 4 feet long and weighs up to 140 pounds. One of the smallest rodents is the pygmy mouse of North America. It is only about 4 inches long, including its tail, and weighs just ¼ of an ounce.

CAPYBARA

The capybara lives in marshy places and feeds on grasses.

› WHEN IS A DOG REALLY A RAT?

A prairie dog is actually not a dog at all. It is a type of rodent, and lives in North America. Prairie dogs live in family groups of one adult male and several females and their young. A group of families makes a vast burrow of connecting chambers and tunnels called a colony.

› CAN FLYING SQUIRRELS REALLY FLY?

No, but they can glide from tree to tree. When the flying squirrel leaps into the air, it stretches out the skin flaps at the sides of its body, which act like a parachute, enabling it to glide gently between branches.

BEAVER LODGE

A beaver lodge is built of sticks behind a dam and has an underwater entrance.

Bears

There are eight species of bear. They range in size from the sun bear, which can weigh less than 110 pounds, to huge polar bears and brown bears. Bears have a large body, stocky legs, a long snout, shaggy hair, and sharp claws.

WHICH IS THE BIGGEST BEAR?

The polar bear of the Arctic is one of the largest bears. Full-grown males are up to 8 feet long. Polar bears are meat eaters and hunt seals, young walruses, and birds.

POLAR BEAR

The polar bear is the world's largest land-living predator.

CAN POLAR BEARS SWIM?

Polar bears swim well and spend long periods in the freezing Arctic water. They are well equipped to survive the cold. They have a dense layer of underfur as well as a thin layer of stiff, shiny outer coat. Under the skin is a thick layer of fat to give further protection.

HOW BIG IS A BABY BEAR?

Although adult bears are large, they have tiny babies. A huge polar bear, weighing more than several people, gives birth to cubs of only about 2 pounds, far smaller than most human babies. Baby pandas weigh as little as 3 ounces.

IS THE GIANT PANDA A BEAR?

For years, experts argued about whether this animal should be grouped with bears or raccoons or classed in a family of its own. Genetic evidence now suggests that the panda is a member of the bear family.

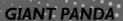

GIANT PANDA

Giant pandas live in bamboo forest reserves in west and central China.

➤ WHAT DO GIANT PANDAS EAT?

The main food of the giant panda is bamboo. An adult panda eats up to 40 pounds of bamboo leaves and stems a day.

TOP ? QUESTION

DO BEARS SLEEP THROUGH WINTER?

Brown bears (below), polar bears, and black bears that live in the far north sleep for much of the winter. Food supplies are poor, so the bears hide away in warm dens and live off their own fat reserves. Before their sleep, the bears eat as much food as they can.

TREE CLIMBER

Like all bears, giant pandas are excellent climbers. They often take shelter in hollow trees and rock crevices.

Wolves and dogs >

The canid family of mammals includes dogs, wolves, foxes, coyotes, dingoes, and jackals. Canids are meat eaters and have long legs for chasing their prey. Their sharp claws and teeth are perfect for slicing flesh.

> HOW MANY KINDS OF DOG AND FOX ARE THERE?

There are about 35 species in the canid family, split between the "true dogs" and the "foxes." True dogs include wolves, jackals, and wild dogs.

DINGO

Dingoes hunt alone, returning to their pack every few days to socialize.

> WHAT IS A DINGO?

Dingoes are Australian wild dogs. They are probably descended from dogs introduced 5,000–8,000 years ago by Aborigines. Nowadays, they hunt mainly sheep and rabbits. A fence of over 3,000 miles has been built across southeastern Australia to keep dingoes out of sheep-grazing land.

➤ WHAT DO FOXES EAT?

Foxes, such as the red fox, are hunting animals. They kill and eat small creatures, including rats, mice, and rabbits. But foxes are very adaptable and will eat more or less anything that comes their way, such as birds and birds' eggs, insects, and even fruit and berries. More and more foxes in cities are feasting on our discarded food from garbage cans and compost piles.

RED FOX PUP

Red fox pups are taken care of by their parents until they reach 8–10 months old.

➤ WHAT IS A COYOTE?

The coyote looks similar to a wolf, with large ears and long legs for running. It lives in North and Central America, where it hunts small mammals, such as squirrels and mice. Coyotes form a small pack but hunt with just one partner.

HOW BIG IS A WOLF PACK?

In areas where there are plenty of large animals to catch, a pack may contain up to 30 wolves. Hunting in a pack means that the wolves can kill prey much larger than themselves, such as moose. A wolf pack has a territory, which it defends against other wolves.

Cats >

There are about 36 species of wild cat, ranging from the tiger to the African wild cat, which is closely related to the domestic cat. Wild cats live in every sort of habitat, from tropical rain forest to desert. There are no wild cats in Antarctica, Australia, or New Zealand.

> WHAT DO LIONS DO ALL DAY?

Like domestic cats, lions are actually asleep for a surprisingly large part of the day. As much as 20 hours a day are spent resting and grooming. The rest of the time is taken up with looking for prey, hunting, and feeding. Lionesses do most of the hunting, then share the catch with the rest of the pride.

TIGER

The pattern of stripes on a tiger's fur is unique. No two tigers have exactly the same pattern.

HUNTING LIONS

Lionesses develop a carefully coordinated group strategy to bring down their prey.

120

➤ WHICH IS THE BIGGEST CAT?

Tigers are the biggest of the big cats. They can measure over 10 feet long, including the tail, and weigh 550 pounds or more. Tigers are becoming very rare. They live in parts of Asia, from snowy Siberia in the north to the tropical rain forests of Sumatra, Indonesia.

➤ WHICH IS THE FASTEST CAT?

The cheetah is the fastest-running cat and one of the speediest of all animals over short distances. It has been timed running at more than 60 miles an hour over a distance of 600 feet—more than twice as fast as humans.

?

TOP QUESTION

WHY DO TIGERS HAVE STRIPES?

A tiger's stripes help it hide among grasses and leaves so it can surprise its prey. Tigers cannot run fast for long distances, so they depend on being able to get close to their prey before making the final pounce. The stripes help to break up their outline and make them hard for prey to see.

SNOW LEOPARD

This big cat hunts alone, sometimes killing animals three times its size.

➤ WHERE DO JAGUARS LIVE?

Jaguars live in the forests of Central and South America. The jaguar is a good climber and often clambers up a tree to watch for prey. It hunts other forest mammals, such as peccaries and capybaras, as well as birds and turtles.

➤ WHAT IS A SNOW LEOPARD?

The snow leopard is a big cat that lives in the mountains of Central Asia. Its beautiful pale coat with dark markings has made it the target of fur poachers. Killing snow leopards for their fur is now illegal, but poaching still goes on.

Elephants

Elephants are the largest land animals. There are probably three species: the African bush elephant, African forest elephant, and Asian elephant. Elephants have tusks, long trunks, flapping ears, and very thick skin.

> HOW LONG ARE AN ELEPHANT'S TUSKS?

An elephant's tusks grow throughout its life, so the oldest elephants have the longest tusks. One tusk in the British Museum in London measures 11 feet.

> WHY ARE BIG EARS USEFUL?

Elephants live in hot climates, so they flap their ears to create a breeze. This breeze cools their surface blood vessels, and the cooler blood is circulated to the rest of the elephant's body.

> HOW MUCH DO ELEPHANTS EAT?

A full-grown elephant eats 170 to 340 pounds of plant food a day. Its diet includes grass, twigs, branches, leaves, flowers, and fruits.

AFRICAN ELEPHANT

An elephant uses its tusks to dig for water, tree pulp, or roots, and to clear its path of trees and branches.

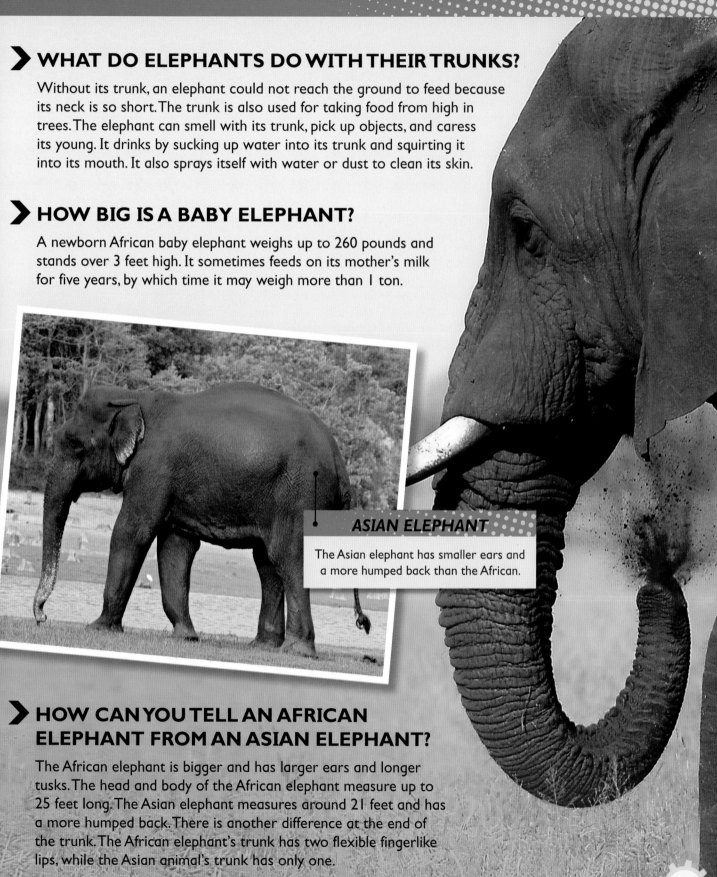

➤ WHAT DO ELEPHANTS DO WITH THEIR TRUNKS?

Without its trunk, an elephant could not reach the ground to feed because its neck is so short. The trunk is also used for taking food from high in trees. The elephant can smell with its trunk, pick up objects, and caress its young. It drinks by sucking up water into its trunk and squirting it into its mouth. It also sprays itself with water or dust to clean its skin.

➤ HOW BIG IS A BABY ELEPHANT?

A newborn African baby elephant weighs up to 260 pounds and stands over 3 feet high. It sometimes feeds on its mother's milk for five years, by which time it may weigh more than 1 ton.

ASIAN ELEPHANT
The Asian elephant has smaller ears and a more humped back than the African.

➤ HOW CAN YOU TELL AN AFRICAN ELEPHANT FROM AN ASIAN ELEPHANT?

The African elephant is bigger and has larger ears and longer tusks. The head and body of the African elephant measure up to 25 feet long. The Asian elephant measures around 21 feet and has a more humped back. There is another difference at the end of the trunk. The African elephant's trunk has two flexible fingerlike lips, while the Asian animal's trunk has only one.

Large animals

After the elephant, the largest land animals are the rhinoceros, hippopotamus, and giraffe. All three live in Africa, while the rhino also lives in Asia. These mammals are plant eaters known as ungulates, which are distinguished by their hoofed feet.

› HOW MANY BONES ARE THERE IN A GIRAFFE'S NECK?

A giraffe has seven bones in its neck, just like other mammals, including humans. But the giraffe's neck bones are much longer than those of other animals, and have more flexible joints in between them.

› HOW TALL IS A GIRAFFE?

A male giraffe stands up to 18 feet tall to the tips of its horns. It has a very long neck, and front legs that are longer than its back legs so that the body slopes down toward the tail. The long neck allows it to feed on leaves that other animals cannot reach.

GIRAFFES

A giraffe's height allows it to watch out constantly for predators. It needs to sleep for only two hours a day.

CAN HIPPOS SWIM?

The hippo spends most of its day in or near water and comes out onto land at night to feed on plants. It is a powerful swimmer and walks on the bottom of the river at surprisingly fast speeds.

HIPPO

Hippos wallow to stay cool in the hot African sun.

WHAT IS AN OKAPI?

An okapi is a relative of the giraffe that lives in the African rain forest. It was unknown until 1900. The male has small horns on its head and a long tongue like a giraffe's, but it does not have a long neck.

IS THE RHINO ENDANGERED?

All five species of rhinoceros are endangered. The Javan rhino is the most vulnerable. Rhinoceroses have been overhunted for their horns, which are valuable in traditional medicine.

WHITE RHINO

The white rhino is actually grayish. It is also known as the square-lipped rhino.

ARE RHINOCEROSES FIERCE?

Despite their ferocious appearance and huge horns, white rhinos are usually peaceful, plant-eating animals. However, black rhinos can be ill-tempered and aggressive. If threatened, one will charge its enemy at high speed. Mothers defending their young can be particularly dangerous.

125

Marsupials >

Marsupials have much shorter pregnancies than other mammals. After birth, the tiny newborns often live in a pouch on their mother's belly. Many of the 330 species of marsupial live in Australia and New Guinea.

> DO ALL MARSUPIALS HAVE A POUCH?

Most female marsupials have a pouch, but not all. Some very small marsupials such as the shrew opossums of South America do not have a pouch. Others, such as the American opossums, simply have flaps of skin around the nipples that the tiny young cling on to.

> IS A KOALA REALLY A BEAR?

No, it's a marsupial and not related to bears at all. Koalas live in Australia in eucalyptus forests. They feed almost entirely on eucalyptus leaves, preferring those of only a few species. A baby koala spends its first six or seven months in the pouch and then rides on its mother's back until it is able to fend for itself. A baby measures around ¾ of an inch at birth.

KOALA
The koala has strong claws to help it hold onto branches as it climbs in search of food.

> HOW MUCH DOES A KOALA EAT?

A koala eats about 18 ounces of eucalyptus leaves every day, which it chews down to a fine pulp with its broad teeth.

PLATYPUS

This unusual mammal hunts in rivers and lakes using its sensitive bill. It feeds on insects, frogs, and shrimp.

> WHAT IS THE SMALLEST MARSUPIAL?

The smallest marsupials are the mouselike ningauis, which live in Australia. They are only about 2 inches long.

WOMBAT

Wombats eat grasses, roots, bark, and herbs.

> IS A PLATYPUS A MARSUPIAL?

No, the platypus is not a marsupial, but it is an unusual animal that lives in Australia. Unlike most mammals, which give birth to live young, the platypus lays eggs. When they hatch, the young suck milk from the mother from special patches of fur.

> WHAT IS A WOMBAT?

A wombat is a small bearlike marsupial with a heavy body and short, strong legs. It digs burrows to shelter in, using its strong teeth and claws. Its pouch opens to the rear so that it does not fill up with earth when the wombat is burrowing.

More marsupials >

More than 200 species of marsupial live in Australia and surrounding islands. There are also over 100 marsupial species in the Americas. Most of these live in South and Central America, with just the Virginia opossum native to North America.

> DO ANY MARSUPIALS SWIM?

The water opossum of South America is an excellent swimmer and has webbed back feet. Strong muscles keep its pouch closed when the opossum is in water.

> WHAT ARE BANDICOOTS?

Bandicoots are a group of small marsupials that live in Australia and New Guinea. Most have short legs, a round body, and a long, pointed nose. They have strong claws, which they use to dig for insects and other small creatures in the ground.

BANDICOOT

The bilbie bandicoot has extremely large ears to hear its insect prey.

> HOW FAST DO KANGAROOS MOVE?

A kangaroo bounds along on its strong back legs at up to 30 miles an hour. It can cover almost 45 feet in one giant bound.

TOP QUESTION

WHAT IS A TASMANIAN DEVIL?

The Tasmanian devil (right) is the largest of the carnivores, or flesh-eating, marsupials. It is about 35 inches long, including its tail, and has sharp teeth and strong jaws. The devil feeds mostly on carrion—the flesh of animals that are already dead—but it does also kill prey, such as birds.

❯ WHY DOES A KANGAROO HAVE A POUCH?

At birth, kangaroos are very tiny and poorly developed. A kangaroo is only about ¾ inch long when it is born. The female kangaroo has a pouch so that its young can complete their development in safety. The tiny newborn, called a joey, crawls up to the pouch by itself and starts to suckle on one of the nipples inside the pouch.

❯ WHAT DO KANGAROOS EAT?

Kangaroos eat grass and the leaves of low-growing plants, just like deer and antelopes do in the northern hemisphere.

RED KANGAROO

The largest kangaroo of all, an adult red kangaroo weighs 200 pounds.

JOEY

Joeys stay in the pouch until they weigh 20 pounds.

Monkeys →

Monkeys are members of the primate group, which also contains tarsiers, lemurs, aye-ayes, lorids, galagos, apes, and humans. Primates have large brains, hands that can form a good grip, and a tendency to walk on two legs.

› HOW MANY KINDS OF MONKEY ARE THERE?

About 260 species in two main groups. One group lives in Africa and Asia. The other group lives in Central and South America.

› WHICH MONKEY MAKES THE LOUDEST NOISE?

Howler monkeys shout louder than other monkeys and are among the noisiest of all animals. Their voices carry for more than 2 miles.

HOWLER MONKEY •

The howler monkey spends most of its time in trees, feeding on leaves and fruit.

MACAQUES

Japanese macaques often bathe in hot springs.

➤ CAN MONKEYS LIVE IN COLD PLACES?

Most monkeys are found in warm areas near to the equator, but some macaque monkeys live in cooler places. The rhesus macaque lives in the Himalayas, as well as in parts of China and India, and the Japanese macaque survives freezing winters with the help of its thick coat.

➤ WHICH IS THE BIGGEST MONKEY?

The mandrill is the largest monkey because it can grow to be 3 feet long. It lives in the tropical rain forests of Central Africa, where it hunts for insects, plants, and small animals. The smallest monkey is the pygmy marmoset of the South American rain forests. It is about 5 inches long, plus tail, and it weighs only between 3 and 5 ounces.

GRIPPING TAIL

A prehensile tail is almost as useful as having a fifth limb.

TOP QUESTION

WHY DOES A MONKEY HAVE A LONG TAIL?

To help it balance and control its movements as it leaps from branch to branch in the rain forest. The tails of some South American monkeys are prehensile—they have special muscles that the monkey can use to twine around branches.

131

Apes >

Apes are probably the most intelligent animals in the primate group. There are three families of apes. One includes all the gibbons. The second contains the gorilla, chimpanzee, and orang-utan. And the third has only one species—humans.

> WHAT DO GORILLAS EAT?

Gorillas eat plant food, such as leaves, buds, stems, and fruit. Because their diet is juicy, gorillas rarely need to drink.

FEMALE GORILLA

Closely related to humans, gorillas are very intelligent.

> WHICH IS THE BIGGEST APE?

The gorilla. A full-grown male stands over 5½ feet tall and weighs as much as 480 pounds. Gorillas live in the forests of West and Central Africa. A family group contains one or two adult males, several females, and a number of young of different ages. The male, known as a silverback because of the white hair on his back, leads the group.

CHIMPANZEE

Chimpanzees show love toward each other and even mourn when a relative dies.

> DO CHIMPANZEES USE TOOLS?

Yes. The chimpanzee can get food by poking a stick into an ants' nest. It pulls out the stick and licks ` off the ants. It also uses rocks to crack nuts, and it makes sponges from chewed leaves to mop up water or wipe its body.

> DO CHIMPS HUNT PREY?

Yes, they do. Although fruit is the main food of chimps, they also eat insects and hunt young animals, including monkeys. They hunt alone or in a group. Groups work together, some driving a couple of animals out of the group and toward other chimps, who make the kill.

> WHERE DO CHIMPANZEES LIVE?

Chimpanzees live in forests and grasslands in equatorial Africa. There is another less familiar chimpanzee species called the pygmy chimpanzee, or bonobo, which lives in rain forests in Congo, Africa. It has longer limbs than the common chimpanzee and spends more of its time in trees.

WHERE DO ORANG-UTANS LIVE?

Orang-utans live in Southeast Asia, in the rain forests of Sumatra and Borneo. This ape has long, reddish fur and spends most of its life in the trees. Fruit is its main food, but the orang-utan also eats leaves, insects, and even eggs and small animals. The orang-utan is active during the day. At night it sleeps on the ground or in a nest of branches in the trees.

Lizards >

Lizards are reptiles, which means that they need to breathe air and they have skin that is covered in scales. Most lizards have four limbs and a tail. Many lizards can shed their tail to escape a predator.

KOMODO DRAGON

No predators in its habitat are large enough to take on the fierce adult Komodo dragon.

> WHICH IS THE LARGEST LIZARD?

The Komodo dragon, which lives on some Southeast Asian islands. It grows up to 10 feet long and hunts animals, such as wild pigs and small deer.

> HOW MANY KINDS OF LIZARD ARE THERE?

There are probably over 3,000 species of lizard. These belong to different groups, such as the geckos, iguanas, skinks, and chameleons. Lizards mostly live in warm parts of the world.

> ARE THERE ANY POISONOUS LIZARDS?

There are only two poisonous lizards in the world, the Gila monster (right) and the Mexican beaded lizard. Both of these live in southwestern North America. The poison is made in glands in the lower jaw. When the lizard seizes its prey and starts to chew, poison flows into the wound, and the victim soon stops struggling.

WHERE DO CHAMELEONS LIVE?

There are about 85 different kinds of chameleon and most of these live in Africa and Madagascar. There are also a few Asian species and one kind of chameleon lives in parts of southern Europe.

WHY DOES A CHAMELEON CHANGE COLOR?

Changing color helps the chameleon get near to its prey without being seen and allows it to hide from its enemies. The color change is controlled by the chameleon's nervous system. Nerves cause areas of color in the skin to be spread out or to become concentrated in tiny dots. Chameleons go darker when they are cold and lighter when they are hot.

WHICH LIZARD SWIMS THROUGH SAND?

The sand skink lives in the sandhills of the southeastern United States. It spends most of its time below the surface, pulling itself through the sand like a swimmer moves through water.

GIVING SIGNALS

Chameleons change color not just as camouflage but as a means of communication.

CHAMELEON

The veiled chameleon can turn bright blue when it is on vivid flowers.

Snakes ➤

Like other reptiles, snakes are covered in scales. All snakes are carnivorous, which means that they feed on other animals. There are about 2,500 species of snake. They live on every continent except Antarctica, but there are no snakes in Ireland, Iceland, or New Zealand.

➤ HOW FAST DO SNAKES MOVE?

The fastest-moving snake on land is thought to be the black mamba, which lives in Africa. It can wriggle along at up to 7 miles an hour.

RATTLESNAKE

If the rattle breaks, a new ring will be added when the snake molts.

➤ WHICH IS THE BIGGEST SNAKE?

The world's longest snake is the reticulated python, which lives in parts of Southeast Asia. It grows to an amazing 33 feet long. The anaconda, which lives in South American rain forests, is heavier than the python but not quite as long. Pythons and anacondas are not poisonous snakes. They kill by crushing their prey to death. A python wraps the victim in the powerful coils of its body until it is suffocated.

➤ WHICH IS THE MOST DANGEROUS SNAKE?

The saw-scaled carpet viper is probably the world's most dangerous snake. It is extremely aggressive and its poison can kill humans. Saw-scaled carpet vipers live in Africa and Asia.

WHY DO SNAKES SHED THEIR SKIN?

Snakes molt, or shed their skin, to make room for growth and because their skin gets worn and damaged. Some snakes, even as adults, shed their skin every 20 days.

> ## ARE ALL SNAKES POISONOUS?

Only about one-third of all snakes are poisonous, and fewer still have poison strong enough to harm humans. Nonpoisonous snakes either crush their prey to death or simply swallow it whole.

CAPE COBRA
The deadly Cape cobra of southern Africa can kill humans with its bite.

SNAKESKIN
Snakes wriggle out of their skin by rubbing against rough surfaces.

> ## WHY DOES A RATTLESNAKE RATTLE?

Rattlesnakes make their rattling noise to warn their enemies to stay far away. The rattle is made by a number of hard rings of skin at the end of the tail that make a noise when shaken. Each ring was once the tip of the tail. A new one is added every time the snake grows and sheds its skin.

Life in the water and air

Whales >

Whales, dolphins, and porpoises belong to the group of marine mammals known as cetaceans. They are highly intelligent and have large tails perfect for swimming. Cetaceans breathe air through the blowhole on the top of their head.

> WHICH IS THE BIGGEST WHALE?

The blue whale is the largest whale, and also the largest mammal that has ever lived. It measures almost 100 feet long. Although it is huge, the blue whale is not a fierce hunter. It eats tiny shrimplike creatures called krill. It may gobble up as many as four million of these in a day.

> WHICH WHALE DIVES THE DEEPEST?

The sperm whale is routinely found at over 3,200 feet beneath the surface of the sea.

> HOW BIG IS A BABY BLUE WHALE?

A baby blue whale is about 26 feet long at birth and is the biggest baby in the animal kingdom.

BALEEN PLATES

A right whale skims the sea for krill, showing its baleen plates.

> HOW DOES A BLUE WHALE FEED?

Hanging from the whale's upper jaw are a lot of plates of a bristly material called baleen. The whale opens its mouth and water full of krill flows in. The water flows out at the sides of the mouth, leaving the krill behind on the baleen for the whale to swallow.

> WHY DO SOME WHALES MIGRATE?

Whales, such as humpbacks, migrate—travel seasonally— to find the best conditions for feeding and breeding. They spend much of the year feeding in the waters of the Arctic and Antarctic, where there is plenty of krill to eat. When it is time to give birth, the humpbacks travel to warmer waters near the equator.

> DO HUMPBACK WHALES SING?

Yes, they do. They make a series of sounds, including high whistles and low rumbles, that may last from 5 to 35 minutes. No one knows why the humpback whale sings, but it may be to court a mate or to keep in touch with others in the group.

HUMPBACK WHALE

Whales often "breach," flinging themselves out of the water and landing with a noisy splash.

More whales

There are two groups of whales: toothed whales and whales that catch food with baleen filters. Dolphins and porpoises are toothed, while blue and humpback whales are baleen whales.

> DO WHALES EVER COME TO LAND?

No, whales spend their whole lives in the sea. But they do breathe air and surface regularly to take breaths.

> IS A DOLPHIN A WHALE?

A dolphin is a small whale. Most of the 32 or so species of dolphin live in the sea, but there are 5 species that live in rivers. The biggest dolphin is the killer whale (left), which grows up to 32 feet long. Dolphins have a streamlined shape and a beaked snout containing sharp teeth.

SPY HOPPING

Dolphins often "spy hop," coming to the surface to look around.

➤ DO WHALES GIVE BIRTH IN WATER?

Yes, they do. The baby whale comes out of the mother's body tail first so that it does not drown during birth. As soon as the head emerges, the mother and the other females attending the birth help the baby swim to the surface to take its first breath.

➤ WHAT IS A PORPOISE?

A porpoise is a small whale with a rounded head, not a beaked snout like a dolphin. There are six species of porpoise. They live in coastal waters in the Atlantic, Pacific, and Indian oceans. Like other toothed whales, the porpoise uses echolocation to find its prey. It gives off a series of high-pitched clicking sounds and the echoes tell the porpoise its prey's direction.

➤ HOW FAST DO WHALES SWIM?

Blue whales can move at speeds of up to 20 miles an hour when disturbed. Some small whales, such as pilot whales and dolphins, may swim at more than 30 miles an hour.

WHAT IS A NARWHAL?

A narwhal is a whale with a single long tusk at the front of its head. The tusk is actually a tooth, which grows out from the upper jaw. It can be as much as 10 feet long. Only male narwhals have tusks. They may use them in battles with other males.

TUSKING

These narwhals are "tusking," or rubbing their tusks together.

COMMON DOLPHIN

Dolphins are fast swimmers and catch squid and fish to eat.

Sharks and rays >

Sharks and rays belong to a group of fish that have skeletons made of cartilage instead of bone. Cartilage is softer and more flexible than bone. Sharks and rays also have much larger brains than other types of fish. Sharks are the ocean's most feared predators.

> HOW MANY KINDS OF SHARK ARE THERE?

There are over 300 different species of shark living all over the world. They range in size from dwarf dogfish measuring only 8 inches long to the giant whale shark, which can grow to 50 feet.

> ARE ALL SHARKS KILLERS?

No, two of the largest sharks, the whale shark and the basking shark, eat only tiny shrimplike creatures. They filter these from the water through strainerlike structures in the mouth.

> HOW BIG IS A GREAT WHITE SHARK?

Great white sharks (right) are mostly about 23 feet long, but some can grow up to 40 feet. They live in warm seas all over the world. Great white sharks are fierce hunters and attack large fish and creatures, such as sea lions and porpoises. Their main weapons are their large, jagged-edge teeth.

TIGER SHARKS

These sharks prey on fish, seals, birds, turtles, and other sharks.

> HOW FAST DO SHARKS SWIM?

A shark is able to swim at speeds of up to 25 miles an hour for short periods.

> DOES A STINGRAY STING?

A stingray gets its name from the sharp spine near the base of its tail. The stingray lives in warm, shallow waters, where its spine can cause a nasty wound if stepped on.

STINGRAY

The blue-spotted stingray is up to 27 inches wide.

Fish

Fish live in all the world's bodies of water, from mountain streams to the depths of the oceans. Fish have streamlined bodies ideal for swimming through water. Most fish are covered in scales to provide protection from predators.

WHAT IS AN ANEMONEFISH?

Anemonefish live in sea anemones that thrive in tropical waters. Sea anemones are related to jellyfish and have a powerful sting. Anemonefish are the only fish that are immune to the poison, so they can hide from predators in their host.

HOW FAST DO FISH SWIM?

The sailfish is one of the fastest-swimming fish. It can move at speeds of more than 70 miles an hour. Marlins and tunas are also fast swimmers. All these fish have sleek, streamlined bodies.

ANEMONEFISH

The clown anemonefish hides among anemone tentacles.

PIRANHA

Piranhas are known for their triangular-shape teeth.

TOP QUESTION

?

WHICH IS THE FIERCEST FRESH-WATER FISH?

The piranha, which lives in rivers in tropical South America, is the fiercest of all freshwater fish. Each fish is only about 10 to 24 inches long, but a shoal of hundreds attacking together can kill and eat a large mammal very quickly. The piranha's weapons are its extremely sharp, flesh-ripping teeth.

> ARE ELECTRIC EELS REALLY ELECTRIC?

Yes, they are. The electric eel's body contains special muscles that can release electrical charges into the water. These are powerful enough to stun its prey.

> WHY DOES A FLYING FISH "FLY"?

A flying fish usually lifts itself above the water to escape from danger. It has extralarge fins, which act as "wings." After building up speed under the water, the fish lifts its fins and glides above the surface for a short distance.

PUFFER FISH

This fish puffs up its body when it is threatened.

> ARE THERE ANY POISONOUS FISH IN THE SEA?

Yes, and the puffer fish is one of the most poisonous of all. It has a powerful poison in some of its internal organs, such as the liver, which can kill a human. Despite this, carefully prepared puffer fish is a delicacy in Japan.

Amphibians >

Unlike other land animals, most amphibians lay their eggs in water. Young amphibians live and breathe in water, before transforming into air-breathing and land-living adults.

> HOW CAN TREE FROGS CLIMB TREES?

Tree frogs are excellent climbers. On each of their long toes is a round sticky pad, which allows them to cling to the undersides of leaves and to run up the smoothest surfaces. Tree frogs spend most of their lives in trees, catching insects to eat, and may only come down to the ground to lay their eggs in or near water.

> WHY DO FROGS CROAK?

Male frogs make their croaking calls to attract females. The frog has a special sac of skin under its chin, which blows up and helps make the call louder.

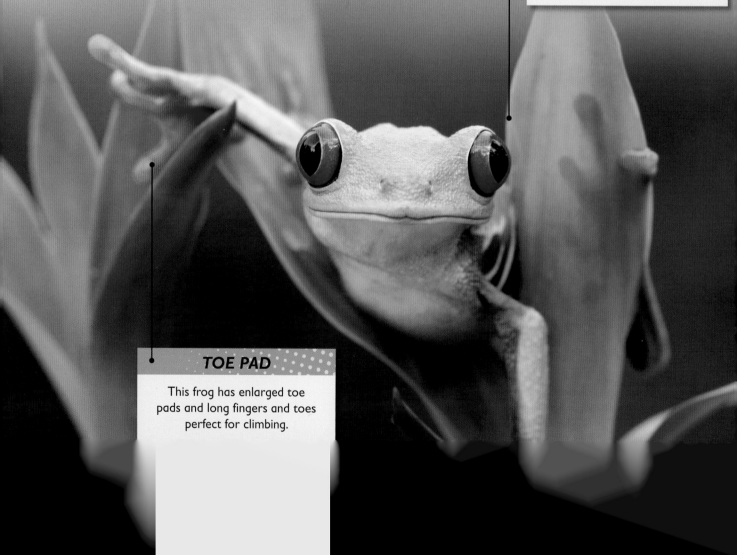

TREE FROG

Tree frogs are tiny creatures, so that their weight can be supported by delicate leaves and twigs.

TOE PAD

This frog has enlarged toe pads and long fingers and toes perfect for climbing.

TADPOLE

As tadpoles mature, they slowly grow limbs.

WHAT IS A TADPOLE?

A tadpole is the larva, or young, of an amphibian, such as a frog or newt. The amphibian egg is usually laid in water and hatches out into a small, swimming creature with a long tail called a tadpole. The tadpole feeds on water plants and gradually develops into its adult form.

WHICH IS THE SMALLEST FROG?

The smallest frog, and the smallest of all amphibians, is the Cuban frog, which measures less than ½ inch long. The tiny gold frog, which lives in Brazilian rain forests, is probably about the same size.

HOW MANY TYPES OF FROG AND TOAD ARE THERE?

There may be as many as 4,000 species of frog and toad. They live on all continents except Antarctica. Most live in areas with plenty of rainfall, but some manage to live in drier lands by sheltering in burrows.

FROGS' EGGS

Many frog species release thousands of eggs at a time.

DO ALL FROGS LAY THEIR EGGS IN WATER?

No, some frogs have very unusual breeding habits. The male marsupial frog (and sometimes the female) carries his mate's eggs in a pouch on his back or hip. The male Darwin's frog keeps his mate's eggs in his vocal pouch until they have developed into tiny frogs.

Crocodiles and alligators >

Crocodiles and alligators are water-dwelling reptiles that live in tropical climates. They have sharp teeth and very powerful jaws. These reptiles also have streamlined bodies and strong legs, so they can move very fast, in and out of water.

> WHAT DO CROCODILES EAT?

Baby crocodiles start by catching insects and spiders to eat. As they grow, fish and birds form a larger part of their diet. Full-grown crocodiles prey on anything that comes their way, even large animals, such as giraffes.

> WHICH IS THE BIGGEST CROCODILE?

The Nile crocodile grows up to 20 feet long, but the Indopacific crocodile, which lives in parts of Southeast Asia, may be even larger.

> HOW MANY TYPES OF CROCODILE ARE THERE?

There are 14 species of crocodile, 2 species of alligator, several species of caiman, and 1 species of gavial. The gavial is very similar to the crocodile and the alligator, with a long, slender snout.

NILE CROCODILE

The crocodile is armored with rows of scales.

DO CROCODILES LAY EGGS?

Crocodiles do lay eggs and they take care of them very carefully. Most female crocodiles dig a pit into which they lay 30 or more eggs. They cover them over with earth or sand. While the eggs incubate for about three months, the female crocodile stays nearby guarding the nest.

❯ ARE CROCODILES AN ANCIENT SPECIES?

Crocodiles have looked the same since the time of the dinosaurs. They are 200 million years old.

❯ HOW CAN YOU TELL A CROCODILE FROM AN ALLIGATOR?

Crocodiles and alligators are very similar, but you can recognize a crocodile because its teeth stick out when its mouth is shut! In alligators, the fourth pair of teeth on the lower jaw disappears into pits in the upper jaw, but in crocodiles, these teeth slide outside the mouth.

ALLIGATOR AGGRESSION

Adult alligators get into frequent battles to defend their territory.

153

Aquatic reptiles >

Crocodiles are not the only reptiles that live in oceans, rivers, and lakes. Aquatic turtles spend most of their lives in water, coming to land to lay eggs. Their bodies are protected by a hard, bony shell. They cannot breathe in water, so must come to the surface for air.

HAWKSBILL TURTLE

The hawksbill turtle is one of the few creatures that feeds mostly on sea sponges.

> WHICH IS THE BIGGEST TURTLE?

The leatherback is the largest of all the turtles. It grows up to 5½ feet long and weighs up to 800 pounds. Leatherback turtles can usually be seen far out at sea.

> ARE THERE SNAKES IN THE SEA?

Yes, there are 50 to 60 species of snake that spend their whole lives in the sea. They eat fish and other sea creatures and all are extremely poisonous. One species, the beaked sea snake, is potentially lethal.

> WHAT DO SEA TURTLES EAT?

Most sea turtles eat a range of underwater creatures, such as clams, shrimp, and snails, but some concentrate on certain foods. For example, the green turtle eats mainly sea grass.

WHERE DO SEA TURTLES LAY THEIR EGGS?

Female sea turtles dig a pit on a sandy beach in which to lay their eggs. They then cover the eggs with sand. When the young hatch, they dig their way out and struggle to the sea.

GIANT FLIPPERS

The female hawksbill uses its flippers for swimming and for digging nests.

> DO TURTLES LIVE IN FRESHWATER?

Yes, there are about 200 species of freshwater turtles living throughout the world's warmer regions.

Polar birds

Few animals are able to survive in the harsh climates of the Arctic and Antarctic. Some hardy birds travel to the polar regions to breed during the relatively warm summers. Some penguin species are able to withstand the bitter Antarctic cold.

WHICH IS THE BIGGEST PENGUIN?

The emperor penguin lives in Antarctica and is the biggest penguin in the world. It stands about 45 inches tall. Like all penguins, it cannot fly, but it is an expert swimmer and diver, using its wings as paddles. It spends most of its life in the water, where it catches fish and squid to eat.

DO ALL PENGUINS LIVE IN ANTARCTICA?

Most of the 18 species of penguin live in or near Antarctica, but some are found in warmer areas, such as around New Zealand. There are no penguins in the northern hemisphere.

HOW FAST DO PENGUINS SWIM?

Penguins can swim at speeds of 8 miles an hour, but they may move even faster for short periods. Some penguins are able to stay under water for up to 20 minutes.

EMPEROR PENGUIN COLONY

Emperor penguins come to land to breed. The female lays an egg that the male keeps warm on his feet for about 60 days until it hatches.

▶ WHICH BIRD MAKES THE LONGEST MIGRATION?

The Arctic tern makes the longest migration journey of any bird. Each year it makes a round trip of 22,000 miles. The birds nest in the Arctic during the northern summer and then travel south to escape the northern winter, spending the southern summer near Antarctica, where food is plentiful.

ARCTIC TERN

These long-lived birds can survive for up to 20 years.

▶ WHICH BIRD HAS THE LONGEST WINGS?

The wandering albatross has the longest wings of any bird. When fully spread, they measure up to 11 feet. This majestic seabird lays its eggs and cares for its young on islands near Antarctica.

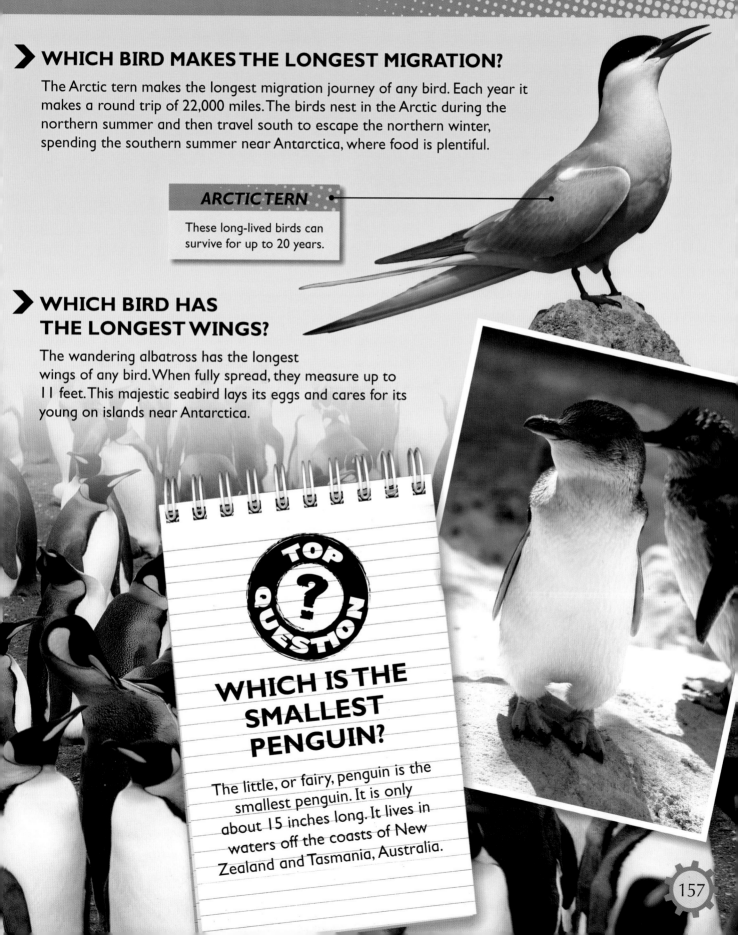

TOP QUESTION

WHICH IS THE SMALLEST PENGUIN?

The little, or fairy, penguin is the smallest penguin. It is only about 15 inches long. It lives in waters off the coasts of New Zealand and Tasmania, Australia.

Birds >

There are around 10,000 different species of bird. They inhabit every one of the world's ecosystems, from deserts to rain forests. Birds have feathers, a beak, and wings. All birds lay hard-shell eggs.

> HOW MANY KINDS OF GULL ARE THERE?

There are about 45 species of gull. They live in all parts of the world, but there are more species north of the equator. Gulls range in size from the little gull, which is only 11 inches long, to the great black-backed gull, a huge 25 inches long. Many gulls find food inland as well as at sea.

GANNET

Gannets are the largest seabirds in the North Atlantic Ocean, with a wingspan of up to 6½ feet.

> HOW DOES A GANNET CATCH ITS FOOD?

The gannet catches fish and squid in spectacular dives into the sea. This seabird flies over the water looking for prey. When it sees something, it plunges from as high as 100 feet above the ocean, dives into the water with its wings swept back, and seizes the catch in its daggerlike beak.

PUFFIN

Puffins have black-and-white plumage and display a colorful beak when breeding.

> IS A PUFFIN A KIND OF PENGUIN?

No, puffins belong to a different family of birds, called auks. They live in the northern hemisphere, particularly around the Arctic. Auks are good swimmers and divers, like penguins, but can also fly, which penguins cannot do.

› HOW MANY SPECIES OF PARROT ARE THERE?

There are about 350 species of parrot, all of which live in the warmer regions of the world. Parrots have a strong, curved beak and many species are brightly colored. Parrots are among the most intelligent birds and can be trained to mimic human speech.

› WHY DOES A PELICAN HAVE A POUCH?

The pelican has a pouch to help it catch fish to eat. When the bird plunges its open beak into the water, the pouch fills up with water and fish. As it brings its head up again, the water drains from the pouch, leaving any fish behind to be swallowed.

MACAWS

The scarlet macaw is a parrot that lives in the forests of Central and South America.

› WHAT IS A TROPIC BIRD?

A tropic bird is a seabird with two very long, central tail feathers. There are three species, all of which fly over tropical oceans.

159

Birds of prey

Birds of prey are hunters, feeding on small animals from insects to fish and mammals. They often make use of keen eyesight and sharp hearing, while their strong beaks and claws are ideal for tearing into flesh.

> DO EAGLES CATCH SNAKES?

Yes, snake eagles feed on snakes and lizards. The rough surface of the eagle's toes helps it hold onto slippery snakes.

GRIFFON VULTURE

The vulture's bald head is ideal for feeding in messy carcasses.

> DO VULTURES HUNT AND KILL PREY?

Vultures do not usually kill their prey. They are scavengers, feeding on animals that are already dead or have been killed by hunters, such as lions. They have strong claws and beaks, and their bald heads allow them to plunge into carcasses without matting their feathers.

> WHICH VULTURE IS A BONE CRACKER?

The bearded vulture picks up bones and drops them from a great height onto rocks. This smashes them open, so the bird can feed on the marrow inside.

PEREGRINE FALCON

This falcon likes to feed on birds, plus small mammals and reptiles.

WHICH IS THE FASTEST BIRD?

As it dives to catch other birds in the air, the peregrine falcon may move at about 200 miles an hour, faster than any other bird. The falcon circles above its victim before making its fast dive and killing the prey on impact.

HOW CAN OWLS HUNT AT NIGHT?

Owls have excellent sight, even in low light, and very sharp hearing. Owls also have special soft-edged wing feathers that make very little noise as they beat their wings, swooping down on their unsuspecting prey.

HOW MANY KINDS OF OWL ARE THERE?

There are 145 species of owl in two families. The barn owl family contains about 10 species and the true owl family about 135 species. Owls live in most parts of the world, except a few islands. They usually hunt at night, catching small mammals, birds, frogs, lizards, insects, and even fish.

More birds of prey

There are about 500 species of birds of prey, including eagles, hawks, buzzards, harriers, kites, falcons, and vultures. All these birds hunt during the day and rest at night. The only nocturnal birds of prey are the owls.

OSPREYS

Ospreys share a small fish in their nest, which is made of a heap of sticks and seaweed.

WHICH IS THE SMALLEST BIRD OF PREY?

The black-legged falconet and the Bornean falconet, of Southeast Asia, both have an average length of 5½–6 inches. They feed on small birds and insects.

WHAT DOES AN OSPREY EAT?

The osprey feeds mostly on fish. When it sees something near the surface, it dives down toward the water and seizes the fish in its feet. The soles of its feet are covered with small spines to help it hold onto the slippery fish.

WHICH IS THE BIGGEST EAGLE?

The biggest eagle in the world is the great harpy eagle, from the rain forests of South America. It is up to 3 feet long. It hunts monkeys and sloths in the trees, chasing them from branch to branch.

> WHICH IS THE BIGGEST BIRD OF PREY?

The Andean condor is the biggest bird of prey in the world. It measures up to 43 inches long and weighs up to 26 pounds. Its huge wingspan is over 10 feet across.

TOP QUESTION?

DO EAGLES BUILD NESTS?

Yes, and the nest, called an eyrie (above), made by the bald eagle is the biggest made by any bird, at up to 18 feet deep. They are used again and again, with the eagles adding more nesting material each year.

ANDEAN CONDOR

The Andean condor's face is nearly featherless, but it has a ruff of white feathers around its neck.

> WHO RULES THE BIRDS?

In Native American mythology, the eagle rules the birds. An eagle kills with the four long, curved claws on each of its feet. It drops down onto its prey, seizes it in its long talons, and crushes it to death. The eagle then tears the flesh apart with its strong hooked beak.

SCIENCE AND TECHNOLOGY

THE WORLD AROUND US

What are things made of?

Everything, from water or air to a whale or a cell phone, is made of tiny particles called atoms. There are over 100 different kinds of atoms, which are in turn made of smaller parts called subatomic particles. Two or more atoms join together to make a molecule. The things around us are solids, liquids, or gases, depending on the arrangement of the atoms and molecules inside them.

BELOW An atom is made of subatomic particles. Particles called electrons circle around the center, called the nucleus.

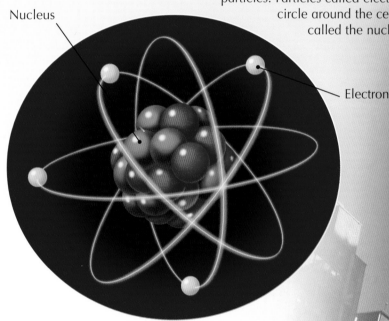

Nucleus

Electron

Buildings need to be made from hard solids, such as stone.

Why are stones hard?

Stones are hard because they are solids. Atoms or molecules in solids are packed tightly and neatly together. This means solids hold their own shape. Some solids are bendable or squishy, such as rubber or feathers. The hardness of a solid depends on how tightly their atoms are held together.

Why is honey runny?

Honey is runny because it is a liquid. The molecules inside a liquid are less tightly packed than they are in a solid, and are not rigidly linked. That is why liquids can flow and take the shape of the container we pour them into. Some liquids are thick, such as honey. Others are thin, such as water.

DID YOU KNOW?
Atoms are so tiny that, even if you put four million atoms side-by-side, they would only be the width of a pinhead!

How do balloons float?

Helium balloons float because the gas inside them is lighter than air. In all gases, molecules move around quickly in all directions. Gases do not stay in one shape as solids do. They can spread out to fill any shape or space. In a hot-air balloon, the air molecules spread out as they heat up. As there are fewer molecules inside the balloon than outside, it floats.

LEFT Hot-air balloons float because the hot air inside them is lighter than the cold air around them.

FORCES AND MOVEMENT

When do things move?

Things only move when a force is applied to them. Forces are pushes or pulls in a particular direction. A flag blows when the wind pushes it. A door opens when you pull it. Animals move when their feet push against the ground, their wings push against air, or their fins push against the water around them.

How do forces work?

Forces work in pairs. They push or pull in opposite directions. When pairs of forces are equal they are said to be balanced. Tug-of-war teams remain still when each pulls with the same strength. A team falls when one side is stronger and the forces are unbalanced. Forces are also balanced when things move at one speed in the same direction.

BELOW A rocket takes off when the force from the engine pushing it up is greater than the force of gravity pulling it down.

Why do things stop moving?

Things slow down and stop because of an opposing force. One of these forces is friction. Friction happens when tiny bumps on two surfaces rub against each other. Rough surfaces, such as concrete, create more friction than smooth surfaces, such as glass. We use high-friction materials such as rubber on shoe soles to stop people from slipping as they walk.

LEFT A bicycle's brakes use high-friction rubber to slow the wheels down.

DID YOU KNOW?
Very fast cars, such as dragsters and rocket cars, need parachutes to slow them down quickly.

How do parachutes work?

Parachutes slow down a person's fall using "air resistance." Air resistance happens when air molecules in front of a moving object squash together and press back against it. The wide area of an open parachute creates a lot more resistance than a person could create with his or her body alone. This reduces the falling speed of the body.

LEFT The wide parachute creates enough air resistance to slow the body's fall.

FORCES IN ACTION

What makes things fall?

Gravity is the force that makes things fall. It is caused by the enormous size of the Earth pulling everything on its surface, or in its atmosphere, toward it. When a stone is dropped in the air, gravity pulls the stone down. Without gravity objects would float in the air.

LEFT A skier is pulled down the hill by the force of gravity.

Why do things float or sink?

Things in water float or sink depending on "buoyancy." Buoyancy is the balance between gravity pulling things down and upthrust. Upthrust is the force of water pushing upward on an object. An aircraft carrier floats because upthrust on its wide hull is greater than the pull of gravity on its great weight.

LEFT Submarines can change their bouyancy to sink or float.

How does a boat's shape help it go faster?

A boat with a sharp, pointed front can go faster than a flat-fronted boat because there is less water resistance. Water resistance is the friction between water and an object moving through it. A boat with a pointed front end allows the water to flow past it easily and smoothly.

DID YOU KNOW?
Maglev trains have no wheels. They move above special tracks using the pushing force of magnetism.

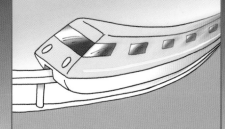

RIGHT Boats with a pointed front, such as this one, are said to be streamlined.

How do refrigerator magnets work?

Refrigerator magnets stick to metal because of the force of magnetism, which pulls them onto the refrigerator. Magnetism can be caused by tiny particles called electrons moving from atom to atom in magnetic metals, such as steel. It can also be caused by a force in a magnet's electrons called spin. A fridge magnet is pulled toward, or attracted to, the metal door of the fridge because of the spin in its electrons.

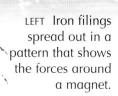

LEFT Iron filings spread out in a pattern that shows the forces around a magnet.

LIGHT AND DARK

Where does light come from?

The Earth's biggest source of light is the Sun. Heat and light energy created by the Sun travels through space in straight lines called rays at almost 187,000 miles per second. The Earth spins around once a day, changing which parts of the globe gets sunlight. This creates day and night. Other things that radiate, or give off, light include electric lightbulbs, candles, and television sets.

ABOVE We make our own light in cities when the Sun goes down at night.

What are shadows?

Shadows happen in places where an object stops light from getting through. Materials that light shines through fully are called transparent. Translucent materials only let a little light through. Opaque materials do not let any light through at all. The shape of a shadow depends on the shape of the object blocking the light. If an object is moved closer to a light source, its shadow gets bigger because it blocks more light rays.

Why do mirrors reflect images?

All surfaces reflect light but, if they are bumpy, the light rays are reflected in all directions. Mirrors are made from very smooth surfaces that reflect the rays back in the same pattern as they hit it, creating a clear image of any object. Words reflected in a mirror appear back to front, as if they were facing away from us and we were looking through the page.

Light

Mirror

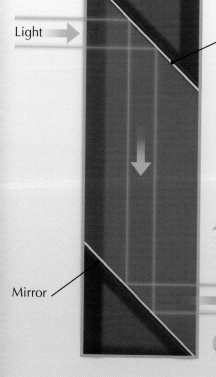

Mirror

ABOVE Periscopes use mirrors to allow people to see things above them.

DID YOU KNOW?
Fireflies flash chemicals that give off light in their bodies to attract mates at night.

How do periscopes work?

Periscopes are devices that use reflecting mirrors in order to see things from a lower level. An angled mirror reflects an image, made up of light, down a tube. A second angled mirror at the bottom of the tube reflects the light again to turn the image back the right way up. Periscopes are often used to see surface ships from underwater submarines, or to see over people's heads in crowds.

COLORS

What are the colors in a rainbow?

There are seven colors in a rainbow and they are always in the same order: red, orange, yellow, green, blue, indigo, and violet. Light from the Sun may look white, but it is actually a combination of many colors. When tiny drops of water in the air split white sunlight into its different colors, we see a rainbow.

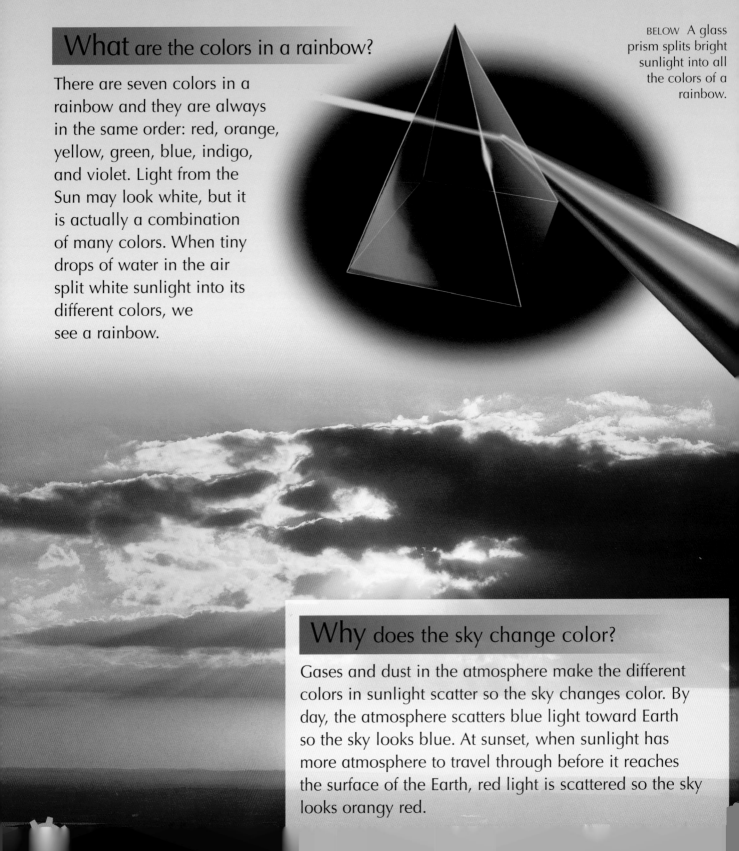

BELOW A glass prism splits bright sunlight into all the colors of a rainbow.

Why does the sky change color?

Gases and dust in the atmosphere make the different colors in sunlight scatter so the sky changes color. By day, the atmosphere scatters blue light toward Earth so the sky looks blue. At sunset, when sunlight has more atmosphere to travel through before it reaches the surface of the Earth, red light is scattered so the sky looks orangy red.

Which colors do we print with?

People print color images and words on paper using just four colored inks: yellow, cyan (blue), magenta (red), and black. Paper is printed with tiny dots of different amounts of each ink. Our brain cannot distinguish the dots we see separately, but instead, blends them together to make different blocks of different colors.

LEFT You can get new colors by mixing other colors together. For instance, mixing blue and yellow makes green.

How do animals use color?

Some animals have colored skin or fur that is similar to their habitats, so they cannot be easily seen. This is called camouflage. Polar bears are white so they can sneak up on seals to catch, and caterpillars are green to to hide on leaves. Other animals use colors so they can be easily seen and avoided. For example, arrow frogs are brightly colored to warn that they are poisonous.

DID YOU KNOW?
Chameleons change color as their mood varies because blobs of pigment (coloring) under their skin get bigger or smaller.

RIGHT Wasps are brightly colored to warn other animals that they have a nasty sting.

SOUND

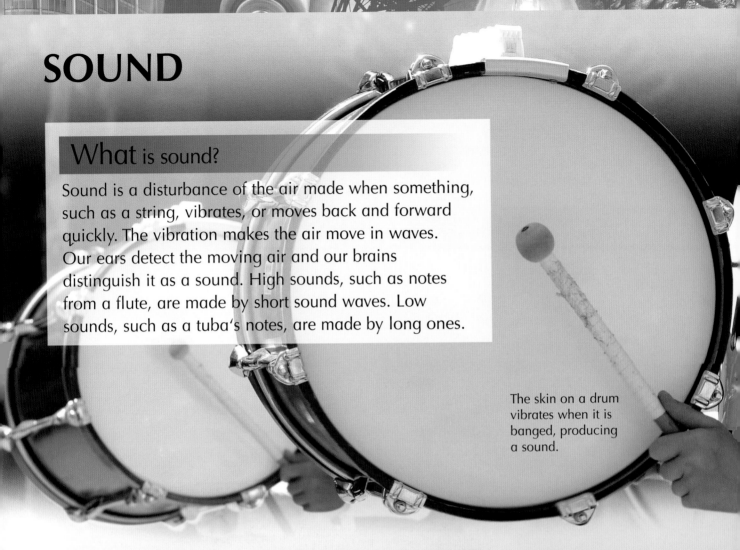

What is sound?

Sound is a disturbance of the air made when something, such as a string, vibrates, or moves back and forward quickly. The vibration makes the air move in waves. Our ears detect the moving air and our brains distinguish it as a sound. High sounds, such as notes from a flute, are made by short sound waves. Low sounds, such as a tuba's notes, are made by long ones.

The skin on a drum vibrates when it is banged, producing a sound.

When do sounds get quieter?

Sound vibrations travel away from the thing that makes them. The vibrations spread out in all directions, like the ripples in a pond after you throw in a pebble. The wider the vibrations spread, the smaller they become and the quieter the sound. Big vibrations, on the other hand, make a lot of energy that pushes a lot of air, creating loud sounds.

How do we measure sounds?

Sound is measured in units called decibels. The quietest sounds, such as a leaf falling, are 0–10 decibels. The loudest sounds, such as a rocket launch, are just less than 200 decibels. Noises above 90 decibels are dangerous to listen to because the strong waves of air can damage the sensitive insides of your ears.

DID YOU KNOW?
It is silent in space because there is no air to convert vibrations into sound waves.

RIGHT We can only just hear leaves falling, but an airplane taking off makes a sound that is so loud it can damage our ears.

What are echoes?

Echoes are the repeated noise we hear when sound waves bounce off solid objects, such as a cliff or the inside of a tunnel. If the object is close by, the waves reflect so quickly we cannot hear the echo as a separate sound. Bats use echoes to get around in the dark. They make squeaks and listen to the echoes to work out how far away things are and how big they are.

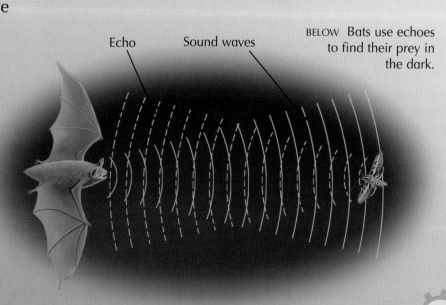

Echo   Sound waves   BELOW Bats use echoes to find their prey in the dark.

177

MATERIALS

Why are saucepans made of metal?

Saucepans are made of metal because most metals heat up quickly. Metal atoms vibrate easily when heated, rapidly passing on the vibrations to atoms around them. This makes metals good conductors (carriers) of heat. Most metals, such as iron, are strong, shiny, hard solids, but metals all have different properties. Aluminum, for example, is light and easily molded.

How is glass made?

Glass is made by heating together sand, ash, and stone in a hot furnace. The molten (liquid) glass is then rolled into sheets, put in a mold, or blown into shapes. It hardens to a transparent solid when it cools. Glass is waterproof and reflects light or lets light through it. It is used to make windows and jars, and also lenses and mirrors.

LEFT The glassmaker dips his blow tube into the molten glass and then blows into it. The glass bulges out and forms a hollow bulb that can be shaped into an object.

178

LEFT Plastic is ideal for making many objects, such as toys, bottles, and chairs.

What are plastics?

Plastics are artificial materials made by heating chemicals found in petroleum (oil). Plastics have many useful properties. They can be molded into different shapes, they do not break easily when dropped, and they are light and waterproof. There are many different types of plastic. For example, Plexiglass is a tough, transparent plastic and polystyrene is a kind of foam used for insulation (to trap heat).

DID YOU KNOW?
Kevlar is a plastic that is five times stronger than steel. It is used to make light bulletproof armor and ropes to moor enormous ships.

When is plastic a problem?

Plastic is a problem because it does not biodegrade, or break down, as food, paper, or wood do. This means that waste plastic piles up in large holes in the ground or floats around oceans, washing up on beaches. Scientists are developing plastics that break down but can still protect and store goods.

179

ROCKS AND SOILS

What are fire rocks?

Fire rocks are "igneous" rocks. These form when hot molten rock called magma forces its way up from deep underground. Sometimes, it reaches the surface as lava from an erupting volcano, where it cools and hardens into igneous rock, such as basalt. Other times, the rock cools more slowly deep underground to form other types of igneous rock, such as granite.

ABOVE When lava cools, the surface is the first part to turn to rock, giving the lava a rocky "skin."

Can rocks change?

Yes, metamorphic rocks are rocks that have "morphed," or changed. The change was caused by extreme heat and the pressure of rocks around them. If you examine metamorphic rock samples closely, you may see some flattened grains of rock. One of the most common metamorphic rocks is marble, which was originally limestone.

ABOVE Coal changes into diamonds when it is put under huge pressure by rock.

Why do some rocks crumble?

Some rocks crumble because they are made of layers of dried mud and sand. These rocks are called sedimentary rocks and include limestone and sandstone. They formed millions of years ago when layers of mud or sand were buried and squashed together underground.

ABOVE Because sedimentary rock is soft, it is easily worn away by the action of wind or water, leaving harder rocks in tall blocks.

DID YOU KNOW?
Fossils, which are the bones and other remains of ancient animals and plants, are almost always found in sedimentary rocks.

Where does soil come from?

Soil comes from rocks and living things. Wind and water break off tiny rock particles from larger rocks. The particles blow or wash onto land, where they mix with tiny pieces of plants and animals. Other animals, such as worms, mix all the pieces together with water and air as they feed, forming soil.

RIGHT Farmers plow the soil to break it up and make it easier for plants to grow in.

FUELS OF THE EARTH

ABOVE Coal formed from trees that grew in swamps in prehistoric times.

What are fossil fuels?

Fossil fuels are oil, natural gas, and coal, which formed from the fossilized remains of plants and animals. In prehistoric times, dead animals and plants became buried inside sedimentary rocks and slowly turned into fossils. Over millions of years, heat and pressure changed the fossils into fuel, in the form of oil, gas, and coal, which can be burned to release heat.

BELOW Oil rigs are platforms in the sea where people drill into the seabed to find oil.

Where do oil and gas come from?

Oil and gas come from rocks deep within the ground. People use very long drills and pipes to release the oil and gas. The rocks are sometimes under land but are often found under the ocean. People drill holes deep into the sea floor and squirt chemicals down the holes to release the fuels. The oil and gas can be made into gasoline, plastic, and other products.

NORTH CORMORANT

When will fossil fuels run out?

The world's oil and gas will run out by 2050, and coal by 2100, if we continue using them at the same rate as today and don't discover any new stores of them in the ground. Fossil fuels are non-renewable, which means that once they are used up they are gone. To save energy, people must use more renewable energy, such as sunlight, wind, or moving water, that will never run out.

DID YOU KNOW?
The biggest oil tanker is longer than the Eiffel Tower is tall and can carry enough oil to fill over 300 Olympic-sized swimming pools!

ABOVE Windmills turning in the wind produce renewable energy.

Can people turn waste into fuel?

Yes, heat energy is released when plant waste, such as unwanted wood or crops, is burned. "Biodegradable waste," such as leftover food, animal manure, scrap paper, and weeds, is degraded, or broken down, by bacteria to make biogas and biofuel. Some crops, such as sugar cane and corn, are specially grown to make biofuel.

ABOVE Pig manure can be made into biofuel.

ELECTRICITY

What is electricity?

Electricity is a type of energy formed from tiny particles inside atoms called electrons. These electrons can move from one atom to another and this movement is electrical energy. Electricity powers many machines, from flashlights and cell phones to televisions and computers. It moves, or flows, into machines through materials called conductors, which include metal wires.

LEFT Lightning, the streaks or flashes of light that can be seen during a thunderstorm, are sparks of electricity.

Where does electricity come from?

Electricity is produced in power plants by machines called generators. Fuel, such as coal, is burned in the power plant to turn water into steam. The steam turns a turbine (a set of large circular blades), which rotates magnets inside the generator, producing electricity. The electricity flows through wires to outlets in our homes.

BELOW Some electricity comes from hydroelectric power plants, where moving water turns the turbines.

ABOVE Batteries make it possible to use a walkie-talkie without plugging it in.

Why do we need batteries?

Batteries are useful for supplying small amounts of power to portable or mobile machines without the need to plug them into outlets in the wall. Batteries are stores of chemicals that create a flow of electrical energy. Some batteries run out when the chemicals are used up, but rechargeable batteries regain their stored electricity when plugged into the outlet.

How do switches work?

Switches work by controlling the flow, or current, of electricity through machines. Electricity can only flow through a circuit, which is a continuous loop of wire. A switch is like a gate that can be opened or closed to break or complete the circuit.

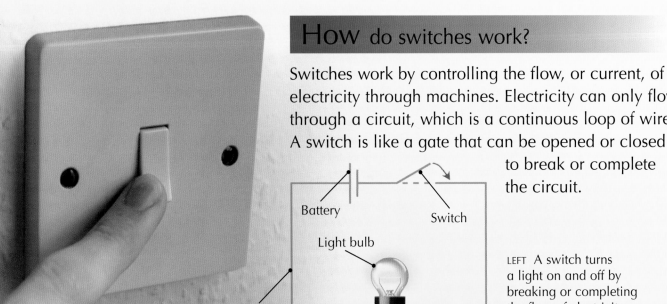

Battery

Switch

Light bulb

Circuit

LEFT A switch turns a light on and off by breaking or completing the flow of electricity through the circuit.

185

MAKING MACHINES WORK

Which machines have motors?

Many machines have electric motors. A motor contains a coil (tightly looped wire) on a shaft in the center of some magnets. When an electric current passes through the coil, the coil becomes magnetized and is repelled by the magnet. This makes the coil rotate and turn the shaft. The turning movement can be used to power machines.

Electric toy train

Drill

ABOVE Many power tools, such as this one used to cut through metal, are driven by motors. Drills and toy trains also contain motors.

Metal filament

RIGHT In an ordinary lightbulb, resistor wires called the filament glow to produce light.

Glass bulb

Why do lightbulbs glow?

Some lightbulbs glow because a thin metal wire, called a filament, inside them converts electrical energy into light energy. Other lightbulbs do not use wires, but make light in a different way. Energy-saving lightbulbs have a special fluorescent coating inside gas-filled glass tubes. When a current passes through the gas, it makes the coating glow.

Metal base that screws into light socket

DID YOU KNOW?

In an ordinary lightbulb, only 10 percent of the energy used produces light. The rest of the energy is wasted as heat.

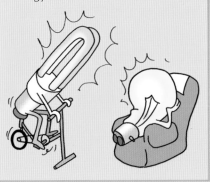

What makes toasters hot?

Toasters get hot because finely coiled wires make heat to toast bread. These finely coiled wires are called resistors. They slow down the flow of electricity. As the movement of electrons is slowed, some of the electrical energy changes into heat energy. Hair dryers work in a similar way. A fan blows air past hot wires to warm the air up.

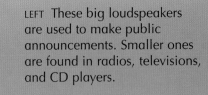

LEFT These big loudspeakers are used to make public announcements. Smaller ones are found in radios, televisions, and CD players.

How do loudspeakers work?

Loudspeakers work by turning electricity into sound. A thin cone of cardboard or plastic, called a diaphragm, vibrates when electrical signals are sent through a wire coil. The loudness and pitch (high or low notes) of the sound produced depend on the size and speed of the vibrations.

DIGITAL TECHNOLOGY

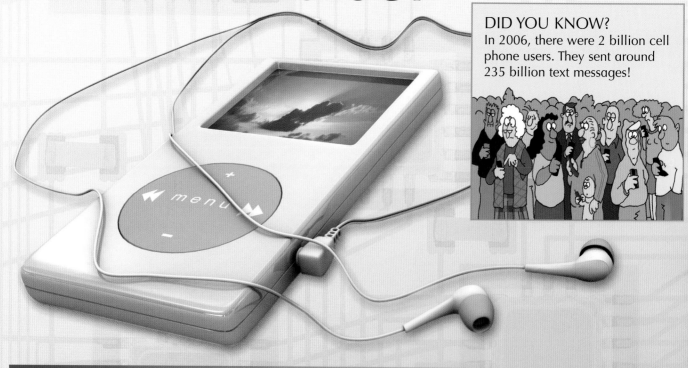

What is digital technology?

Digital technology includes computers, digital cameras, MP3 players, and cell phones. These record, store, send, and process electronic signals as digital information. "Digital" means that the electrical signals are either "on" ("1") or "off" ("0"). The 1s and 0s form a code that can represent any type of information.

BELOW Many microchips are smaller than a half-inch square.

How do microchips work?

Microchips work using tiny electrical circuits. The circuits are built on paper-thin chips of silicon, a material that is very good at conducting electricity (allowing electricity to pass through it). A single microchip can contain thousands of circuits, allowing it to process lots of digital information. Because of microchips, computers and other digital devices can be small and light.

Where can you use the Internet when you are out?

Laptops can connect to the Internet in most places because they are "wireless." This means they have a special antenna that receives radio signals. The computer converts the signals into web pages or e-mails. Because laptops don't need to be plugged in, people can use them on the move.

BELOW Wireless laptops can connect to the Internet in airports, hotels, and even on the beach.

BELOW Robots, such as this toy, work using digital technology.

Will we have robots in the future?

Perhaps, in the future, many of us will have robots in our homes to do the cleaning and cooking and answer the door. There may even be robot cars that drive themselves along preprogrammed routes. But we are already using robots. For example, in some factories, special robots make the cars and, in some hospital operating rooms, robots even help the surgeons perform delicate surgery.

189

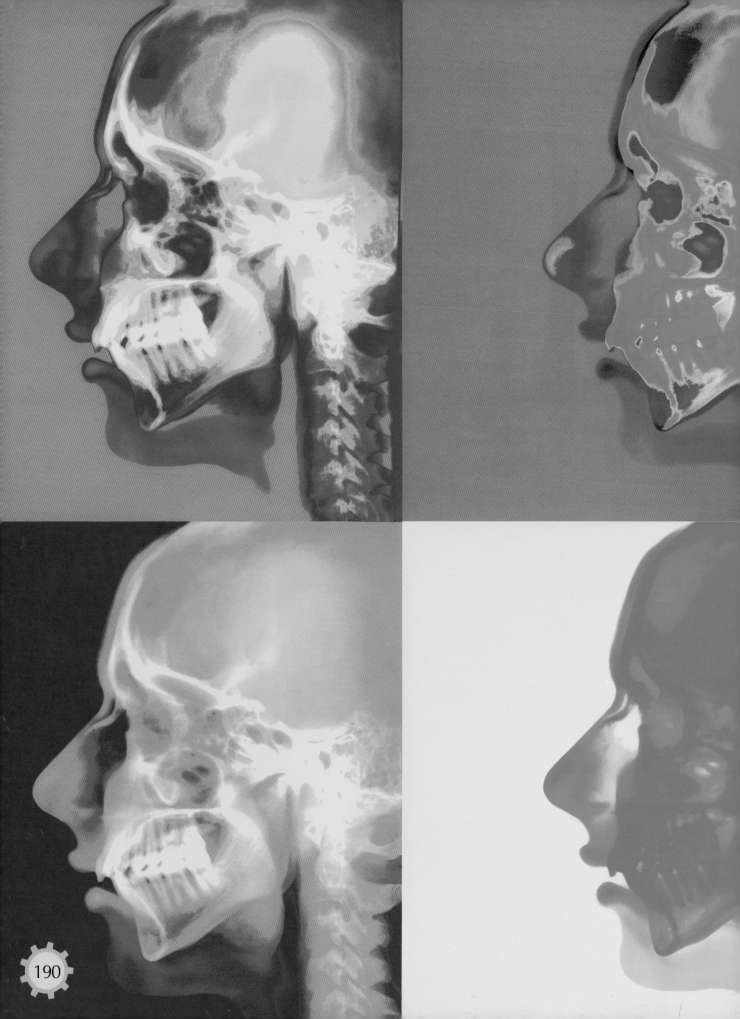

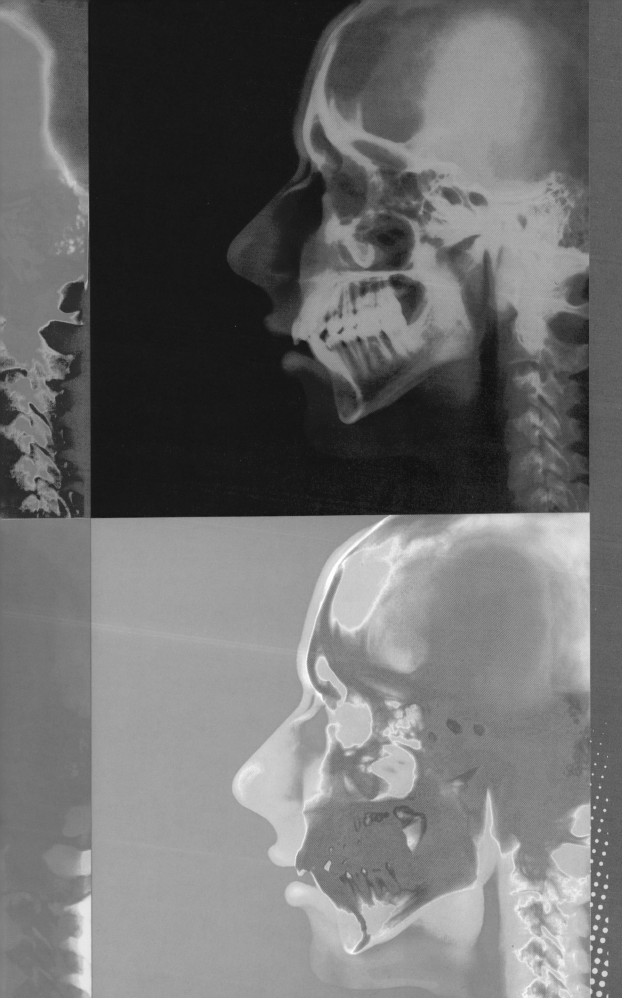

Skin, hair, and nails >

Skin, hair, and nails are part of the body's defenses. Skin forms a protective barrier. Hair keeps us warm. Nails protect our fingers and toes, as well as help us to grasp objects. Skin, hair, and nails contain keratin, a protein that makes them strong.

> WHAT DOES SKIN DO?

Skin stops the moisture inside the body from drying out and prevents germs from getting in. Tiny particles of melanin help to shield your body from the harmful rays of the sun. The more melanin you have, the darker your skin, and the better protected you are.

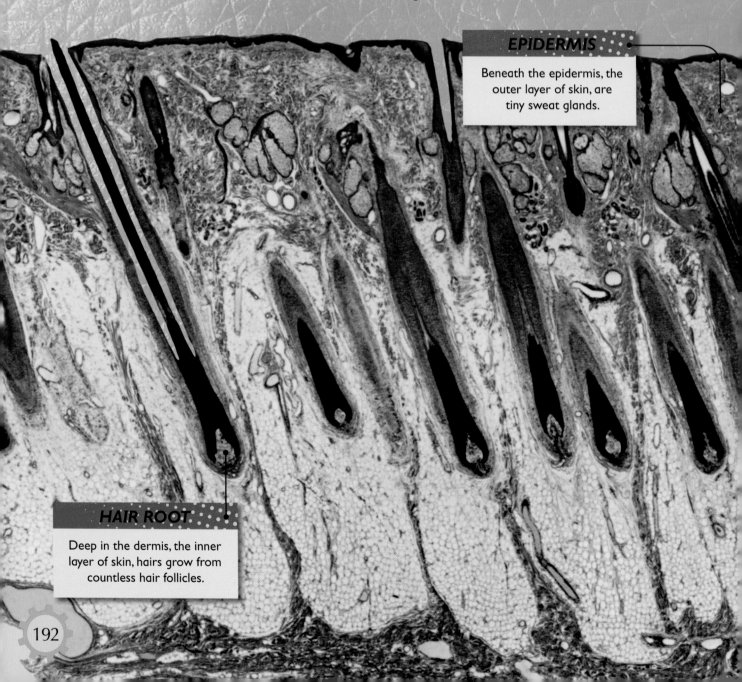

EPIDERMIS

Beneath the epidermis, the outer layer of skin, are tiny sweat glands.

HAIR ROOT

Deep in the dermis, the inner layer of skin, hairs grow from countless hair follicles.

❯ WHY DOES HAIR FALL OUT?

On average, hair lasts for 2–6 years. Every day you lose about 60 hairs, but since you have about 100,000 on your scalp, you hardly notice. After a while, new hairs grow from hair follicles.

MAGNIFIED HAIR

The hair shaft is protected by a hard outer layer.

❯ WHAT GIVES HAIR ITS COLOR?

The color of your hair is determined mainly by the pigment (colored substance) it contains. Hair color depends on melanin, which is a pigment in two forms: one lighter, causing blond or red hair, the other darker, causing brown or black hair.

❯ WHY DOES SKIN HAVE PORES?

Skin has tiny holes, called sweat pores, to let out sweat. When you are too hot, glands pump out sweat, or water, which cools you as it evaporates.

❯ HOW FAST DO NAILS GROW?

A fingernail grows about one twenty-fifth of an inch every 7 days. As new nail tissue forms behind the cuticle, under the skin, it pushes the older nail along.

FINGERPRINT

The uniqueness of fingerprints has led to their being used for identification.

TOP ? QUESTION

ARE FINGERPRINTS UNIQUE?

Yes! A fingerprint is made by thin ridges of skin on the tip of each finger and thumb. The ridges form a pattern of lines, loops, or whorls, and no two people have the same pattern.

The skeleton ➤

Bones provide a strong framework that supports the body and protects the brain, lungs, and other vital organs. You can move and bend different parts of the body because the bones meet at joints.

➤ WHAT IS A JOINT?

Where two bones meet, their ends are shaped to make different kinds of joints. Each kind of joint makes a strong connection and allows a particular kind of movement. For example, the knee is a hinge joint that lets the lower leg move only back and forward. The hip is a ball-and-socket joint that allows you to move your thigh in a circle.

THE SKELETON

All the bones together are called the skeleton. An adult has about 206 bones.

➤ WHY DON'T JOINTS SQUEAK?

Joints are cushioned by soft, squashy cartilage. Many joints also contain synovial fluid, which works like oil to keep them moving smoothly and painlessly.

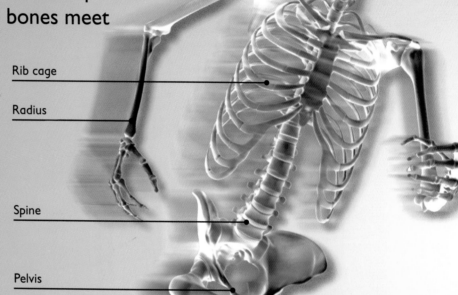

Skull

Rib cage

Radius

Spine

Pelvis

Femur (thighbone)

Patella (kneecap)

Tibia (shin)

Fibula

Metatarsals (foot bones)

BROKEN BONE

Bones can break because of a fall or accident. A break will mend fully in up to 18 months.

HOW MANY VERTEBRAE ARE THERE IN THE SPINE?

A vertebra is a knobbly bone in your spine. The 33 vertebrae fit together to make a strong pillar, the spine, which carries much of your weight.

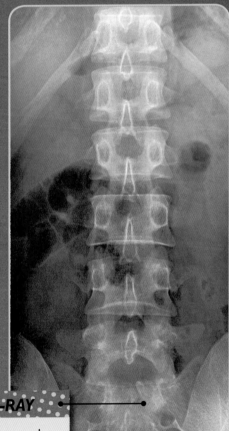

> ## WHICH IS THE LONGEST BONE?

The femur, or thighbone, in the upper part of the leg is the longest bone in the body. It accounts for more than a quarter of an adult's height.

> ## WHAT IS INSIDE A BONE?

Inside the larger bones is a crisscross honeycomb. Blood vessels weave in and out of the bone, keeping the cells alive.

> ## WHAT ARE LIGAMENTS?

They are strong, flexible straps that hold together the bones in a joint. Nearly all the body's joints have several ligaments.

VERTEBRAE X-RAY

The discovery that X-rays can be used to photograph bones was made over 100 years ago.

Muscles >

The skeleton is covered with muscles that move your bones and give your body its shape. Muscles in the legs allow us to run, jump, and kick. Different kinds of muscles make the heart beat and move food through the intestines.

> HOW DO MUSCLES WORK?

Muscles work by contracting. Each muscle is connected to at least two bones. When they contract, muscles get shorter and thicker and so they pull the bones together, causing the body to move.

> WHICH IS THE BIGGEST MUSCLE?

The biggest muscle is the gluteus maximus in the buttock. You can use it to straighten your leg when you stand up, and it makes a comfortable pillow to sit on.

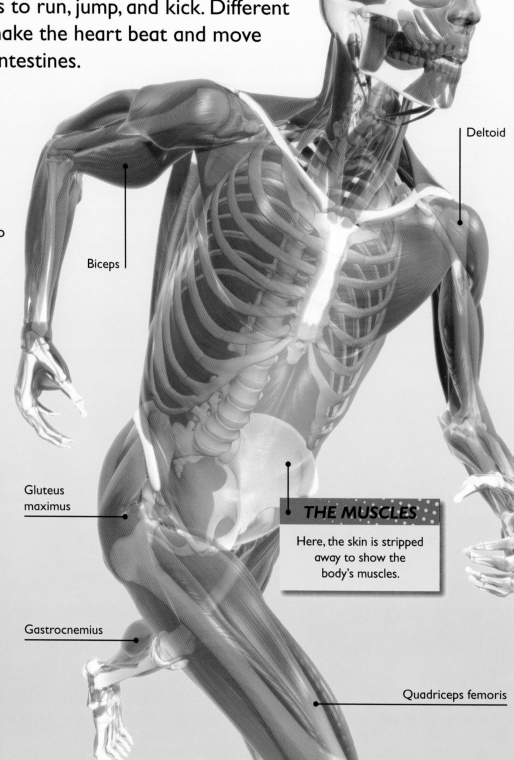

Deltoid

Biceps

Gluteus maximus

Gastrocnemius

THE MUSCLES

Here, the skin is stripped away to show the body's muscles.

Quadriceps femoris

WHY DOES EXERCISE MAKE MUSCLES STRONGER?

A muscle is made of bundles of fibers that contract when you use the muscle. The more you use the muscle, the thicker the fibers become. They contract more effectively, which means the muscle is stronger.

❯ WHY DO MUSCLES WORK IN PAIRS?

Because muscles cannot push, they can only pull. For example, to bend your elbow, you tighten the biceps muscle at the front of your upper arm. To straighten the elbow again, you relax the biceps and tighten the triceps muscle at the back of your upper arm.

❯ WHAT IS A TENDON?

A tendon is like a rope that joins a muscle to a bone. If you bend and straighten your fingers, you can feel the tendons in the back of your hand. The body's strongest tendon is the Achilles tendon, which is above your heel.

❯ HOW MANY MUSCLES ARE THERE IN THE BODY?

You have about 650 muscles that work together. Most actions—including walking, swimming, and smiling—involve dozens of muscles.

STRETCHING

Regular stretching of muscles can make them more flexible.

197

The nervous system ➤

Nerves carry information and instructions to and from the brain. Sensory nerves bring information from the eyes, ears, and other sense organs to the brain. The motor nerves control the muscles, telling them when to contract.

SPINAL CORD

The spinal cord runs through the center of the spine.

➤ HOW DOES SMELL WORK?

A smell is made by tiny particles in the air. When you breathe in, these particles dissolve in mucus in the nose. Smell receptors in the nose respond to this and send a message to the brain.

NERVOUS SYSTEM

Hundreds of nerves reach out to all parts of the body. They are connected to the brain by the spinal cord.

➤ WHAT ARE THE BODY'S FIVE MAIN SENSES?

The five main senses are seeing, hearing, smelling, tasting, and touching. Each sense has a special part of the body, called a sense organ, which reacts to a particular kind of stimulus. For example, eyes react to light and ears react to sound.

➤ HOW DOES TOUCH WORK?

There are many different kinds of sense receptors in the skin, which between them react to touch, heat, cold, and pain. The brain puts together all the different messages to tell you if something is shiny, wet, cold, and many other things.

➤ CAN BLIND PEOPLE USE TOUCH TO READ?

Yes. Blind people can run their fingertips over Braille (right)— a pattern of raised dots that represent different letters.

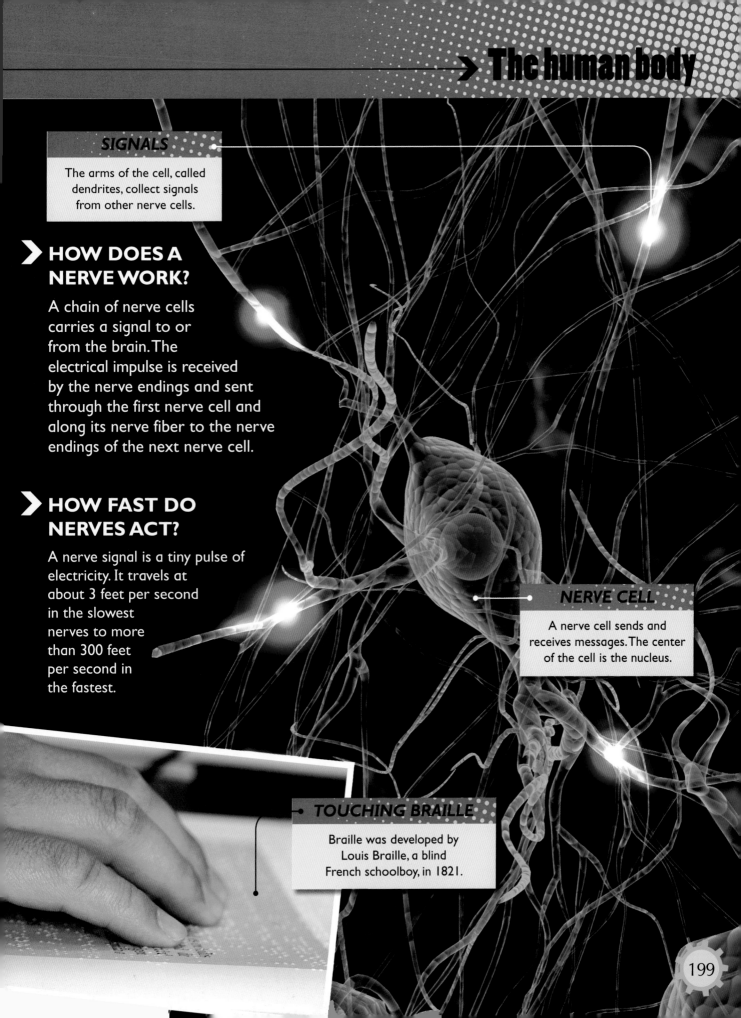

SIGNALS

The arms of the cell, called dendrites, collect signals from other nerve cells.

HOW DOES A NERVE WORK?

A chain of nerve cells carries a signal to or from the brain. The electrical impulse is received by the nerve endings and sent through the first nerve cell and along its nerve fiber to the nerve endings of the next nerve cell.

HOW FAST DO NERVES ACT?

A nerve signal is a tiny pulse of electricity. It travels at about 3 feet per second in the slowest nerves to more than 300 feet per second in the fastest.

NERVE CELL

A nerve cell sends and receives messages. The center of the cell is the nucleus.

TOUCHING BRAILLE

Braille was developed by Louis Braille, a blind French schoolboy, in 1821.

The brain →

Your brain controls your body, keeping the vital organs working, collecting information from the senses, and sending messages to the muscles. The brain also controls everything you think and feel, as well as storing memories of the past.

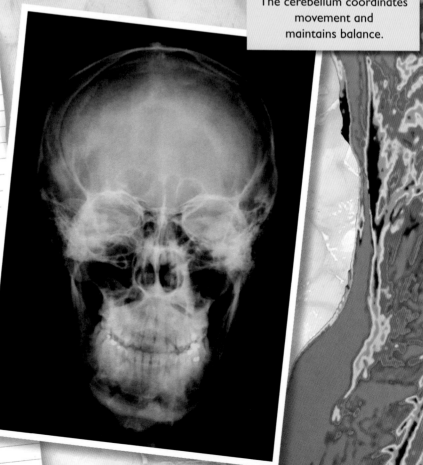

CORTEX

This part of the cerebral cortex controls vision and recognition of colors.

❯ WHAT DOES THE CEREBRAL CORTEX DO?

The cortex is the wrinkly top part of the brain. It controls all the brain activity that you are aware of—seeing, thinking, reading, feeling, and moving. Only humans have such a large and well-developed cerebral cortex. Different parts of the cortex deal with different activities. The left side controls the right side of the body, while the right side of the cortex controls the left side of the body.

CEREBELLUM

The cerebellum coordinates movement and maintains balance.

TOP
?
QUESTION

WHAT DOES THE SKULL DO?

The skull is a hard covering of bone that protects the brain like a helmet. All the bones of the skull except the lower jaw are fused together to make them stronger.

WHY DO YOU REMEMBER SOME THINGS AND FORGET OTHERS?

You usually remember things that are important to you in some way. Some things need to be remembered for only a short while. For instance, you might look up a telephone number, keep it in your head while you dial, and then forget it.

HYPOTHALAMUS

The hypothalamus controls hunger, thirst, and body temperature.

WHY ARE SOME PEOPLE LEFT-HANDED?

Most people are right-handed—the left side of their brain is dominant. In left-handed people, the right side of the brain is dominant. The part of the brain that controls speech is usually on the dominant side.

WHY DO SOME PEOPLE SLEEPWALK?

People may walk in their sleep because they are worried or anxious. If someone is sleepwalking, you should gently take them back to bed.

SLEEPING

The brain blocks most incoming signals while you sleep, unless they are so strong that they wake you up.

WHY DO YOU NEED TO SLEEP?

The truth is that scientists don't yet really know! Sleeping performs some mental function still to be identified. A ten year old sleeps an average of 9 or 10 hours a night, but sleep time can vary between 4 and 12 hours.

The eyes >

You see an object when light bounces off it and enters your eyes. The black circle in the middle of the eye is called the pupil. Light passes through the pupil and is focused by the lens onto the retina at the back of the eye. The retina sends signals to the brain.

> HOW DO YOU SEE COLOR?

Different nerve cells in the retina, called cones, react to the colors red, blue, and green. Together they make up all the colors. The cones only work well in bright light, which is why you can't see color when it gets dark.

THE EYE

The eye is protected by the eyelid. The eyelashes prevent dust and dirt from entering.

Eyelashes

Sclera (white of the eye)

Iris

> WHY DO YOU BLINK?

You blink to clean your eyes. Each eye is covered with a thin film of salty fluid, so every time you blink, the eyelid washes the eyeball and wipes away dust and germs. The water drains away through a narrow tube into the nose.

Tear duct

Pupil

➤ WHY DO YOU HAVE TWO EYES?

Two eyes help you to judge how far away something is. Each eye gets a slightly different picture, which the brain combines into a single three-dimensional or 3D, picture—one that has depth as well as height and breadth.

➤ WHY DOES THE PUPIL CHANGE SIZE?

The pupil becomes smaller in bright light to stop too much light from damaging the retina. In dim light, the pupil opens to let in more light. The iris is a circular muscle that controls the size of the pupil.

EYEBALL

Photoreceptors in the retina send signals along the optic nerve to the brain.

HOW BIG IS AN EYEBALL?

An adult eyeball has a diameter of about an inch, but most of the eyeball is hidden inside your head.

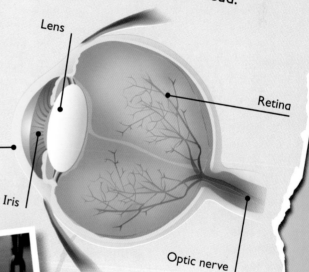

Lens

Retina

Iris

Optic nerve

➤ WHY DO PEOPLE HAVE DIFFERENT COLORED EYES?

The iris is the colored ring around the pupil. The color is made by a substance called melanin. Brown irises have a lot of melanin, while blue irises have a little. Very occasionally, someone has irises of different colors (left).

The ears >

Sound reaches your ears as vibrations in the air. The vibrations travel to the eardrum, which makes the bones in the middle ear vibrate, too. These pass the vibrations to the fluid around the cochlea in the inner ear. Nerve endings in the cochlea send signals to the brain.

> HOW DO EARS HELP YOU TO BALANCE?

Three tubes in the inner ear, called the semicircular canals, are filled with fluid. As you move, the fluid inside them moves. Nerves in the lining of the tubes detect changes in the fluid and send signals to the brain.

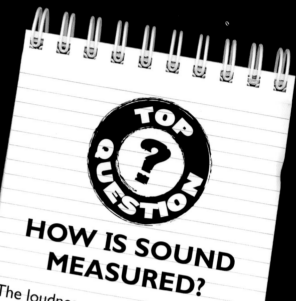

TOP QUESTION

HOW IS SOUND MEASURED?

The loudness of a sound is measured in decibels. The sound of a pin dropping is less than 10 decibels, while a personal stereo makes about 80 decibels. A noise over 120 decibels can damage your hearing.

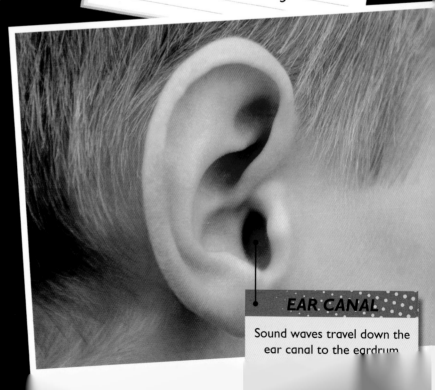

BALANCING

A gymnast balances with the help of semicircular tubes in the inner ear.

EAR CANAL

Sound waves travel down the ear canal to the eardrum

➤ WHY DO YOU GET DIZZY?

If you spin around and around and then stop, the world seems to continue spinning. This is because the fluid in the semicircular canals is still moving as though you were still spinning.

INNER EAR

The cochlea is filled with fluid and lined with auditory cells, which take signals to the brain.

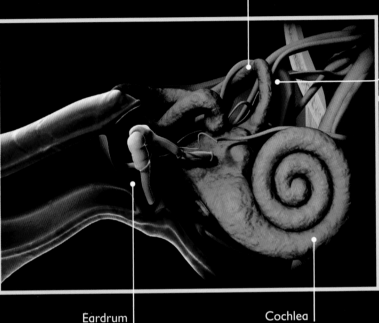

Semicircular canals

Eardrum

Cochlea

OUTER EAR

The outer ear is known as the auricle, or pinna.

➤ WHAT IS EARWAX?

This yellow-brown wax is made by glands in the skin lining the ear canal. Wax traps dirt and germs and is slowly pushed out of the ear.

➤ WHY DO YOU HAVE TWO EARS?

Two ears help you to detect which direction sounds are coming from.

➤ WHY DO YOUR EARS POP?

If you are flying in an aircraft and it changes height quickly, you may go a little deaf, because the air inside and outside the eardrum are at different pressures. Your ears "pop" when the pressures become equal again.

The digestive system >

The digestive system breaks down food into simple nutrients that the body can absorb. The process starts when we chew and swallow food, continues in the stomach and intestines, and ends when waste products are expelled from the body as feces.

> WHAT HAPPENS TO THE FOOD WE EAT?

After it is swallowed, food goes down the esophagus into the stomach. Here it is broken down into a soupy liquid, before being squeezed through a coiled tube called the small intestine. The nourishing parts of the food are absorbed into the blood and the rest passes into the large intestine. About 24 hours after swallowing, the waste, called feces, is pushed out of the body.

> HOW DO YOU DETECT TASTE?

As you chew, tiny particles of food dissolve in saliva and trickle down to the taste buds on the tongue. The taste receptors react and send messages about the taste to the brain.

TASTE BUDS

The tongue has about 10,000 microscopic taste buds. Buds on different parts of the tongue react to different tastes.

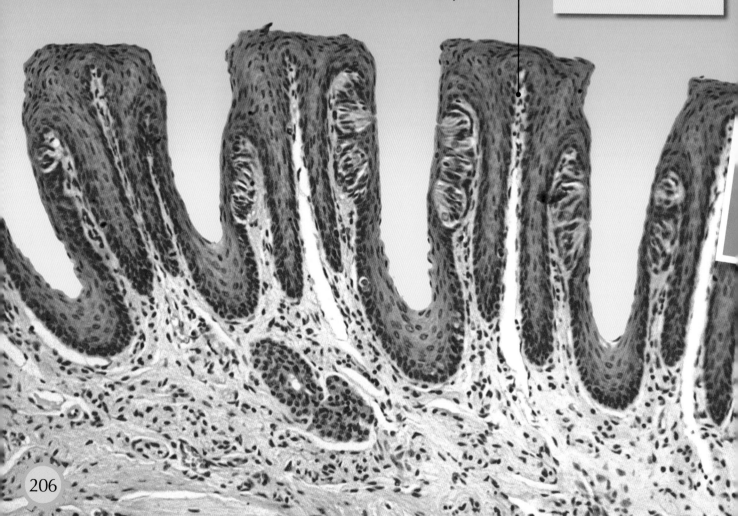

> WHY DOES VOMIT TASTE REALLY SOUR?

When you vomit, you bring partly digested food into your mouth. It is sour because it is mixed with acid made by the stomach lining. The acid helps to break down food into smaller pieces.

> WHAT IS THE EPIGLOTTIS?

The epiglottis is a kind of trap door that closes off your windpipe when you swallow. It stops food from going down into the lungs, rather than down the esophagus to the stomach.

CHEWING

When you chew food, it becomes a mushy ball, ready to travel down the esophagus.

HOW LONG ARE THE INTESTINES?

The small intestine is more than three times as long as the whole body! In an adult this is about 20 feet. The large intestine is a further 5 feet, and the whole tube from mouth to anus measures around 30 feet.

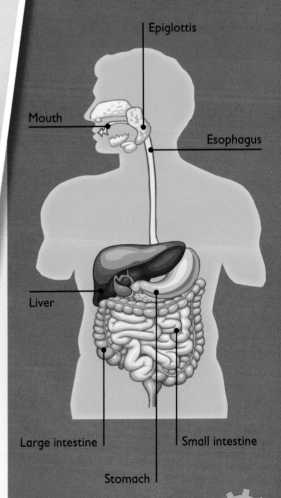

Epiglottis

Mouth

Esophagus

Liver

Large intestine

Small intestine

Stomach

> WHY ARE TEETH DIFFERENT SHAPES?

Different teeth do different jobs to help you to chew up food. The broad, flat teeth at the front slice through food when you take a bite. They are called incisors. The pointed canine teeth grip and tear chewy food, such as meat. The large premolars and molars grind the food between them into small pieces.

207

The lungs and breathing ➤

The air contains oxygen, which the body needs to stay alive. When you breathe in, you pull air through the mouth or nose into the windpipe and down to the lungs. Here the oxygen is passed into the blood, then carried to all parts of the body.

➤ HOW LONG CAN YOU HOLD YOUR BREATH?

You can probably hold your breath for about a minute. The longer you hold your breath, the higher the carbon dioxide level in your blood rises, and the more you feel the need to breathe out.

➤ WHAT HAPPENS TO AIR IN THE LUNGS?

The air you breathe in travels from the windpipe into bronchioles, or tiny tubes, in the lungs. At the end of each bronchiole are minute balloons called alveoli. As these balloons fill with air, oxygen passes from them into the blood vessels that surround them. The blood then carries the oxygen around the body. At the same time, waste carbon dioxide passes out of the blood and into the lungs. It leaves the body in the air you breathe out.

BREATH CLOUD

The air you breathe out contains water vapor. On a cold day, this condenses into a mist of tiny water droplets.

➤ WHY DO YOU COUGH?

You cough when mucus, dust, or other particles clog the air passages between your nose and lungs. The sudden blast of air helps to clear the tubes.

▶ HOW DO YOU TALK?

When you breathe out, the air passes over the vocal cords in the larynx, or voice box, in the neck. When the cords vibrate, they make a sound. Changing the shape of your lips and tongue makes different sounds, which can be put together into words.

▶ WHY DOES RUNNING MAKE YOU PUFF?

Muscles use up oxygen as they work. When you run, your muscles are working hard and need extra oxygen. Puffing makes you breathe in up to 20 times more air to supply your muscles with the oxygen they need.

LUNGS

Inhaled air moves through the windpipe into the bronchial tubes, which divide into tiny tubes called bronchioles.

TOP QUESTION ?

WHY DO THE LUNGS HAVE SO MANY ALVEOLI?

In order to provide a huge surface across which oxygen and carbon dioxide can move in and out of the blood. In fact, the lungs have more than 700 million alveoli.

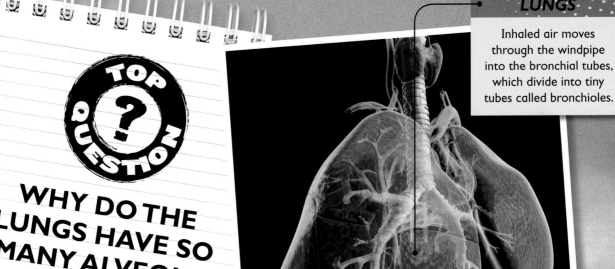

The heart and blood >

The heart's job is to pump blood to the lungs and then all around the body. The right side of the heart takes in blood from the body and pumps it to the lungs. The left side takes blood filled with oxygen from the lungs and pumps it around the body.

> HOW OFTEN DOES THE HEART BEAT?

A child's heart usually beats about 80 times a minute, a little faster than an adult's (70 times a minute). When you run or do something strenuous, your heart beats faster to send more blood to the muscles.

RED BLOOD CELL

Each tiny drop of blood contains up to 5 million red blood cells. These are the most common type of blood cell.

> WHY IS BLOOD RED?

Blood gets its color from billions of red blood cells. These cells contain a substance called hemoglobin, which absorbs oxygen in the lungs. Blood that is rich in oxygen is bright red, and as it is pumped around the body, the oxygen is gradually taken up by the body's cells. By the time the blood returns to the heart, it is a darker, more rusty red.

WHAT DO WHITE BLOOD CELLS DO?

They surround and destroy germs and other intruders that get into the blood.

DEFENSE

White blood cells are part of the immune system, protecting us from infection.

➤ WHAT IS PLASMA?

Just over half the blood is a yellowish liquid called plasma. It is mainly water with molecules of digested food and essential salts dissolved in it.

➤ WHAT IS THE HEART MADE OF?

A special kind of muscle, called cardiac (heart) muscle, which never gets tired.

Artery

Vein

➤ WHAT IS A CAPILLARY?

Blood travels around the body through tubes called arteries and veins. These branch off into smaller tubes that reach every cell of the body. Capillaries are the tiniest blood vessels of all. Most capillaries are thinner than a single hair.

CARDIOVASCULAR SYSTEM

Oxygen-rich blood leaves the heart along arteries (red in this diagram) and used blood returns along veins (in blue).

The kidneys and liver >

The kidneys filter the blood to remove wastes and extra water and salts. The liver is a chemical factory that does more than 500 different jobs, including the processing of food and the removal of wastes and poisons from the blood.

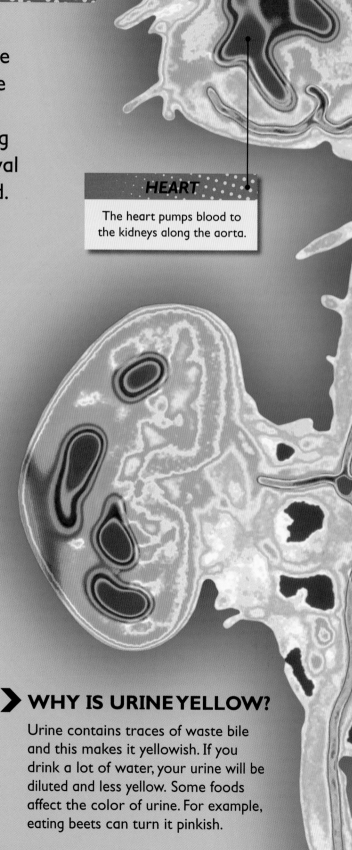

HEART
The heart pumps blood to the kidneys along the aorta.

> WHAT IS URINE?

Each kidney has about a million tiny filters, which between them clean about a quarter of your blood every minute. The unwanted substances combine with water to make urine, which trickles down to the bladder.

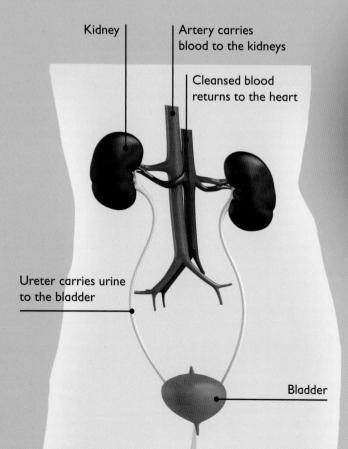

Kidney

Artery carries blood to the kidneys

Cleansed blood returns to the heart

Ureter carries urine to the bladder

Bladder

> WHY IS URINE YELLOW?

Urine contains traces of waste bile and this makes it yellowish. If you drink a lot of water, your urine will be diluted and less yellow. Some foods affect the color of urine. For example, eating beets can turn it pinkish.

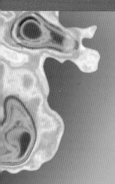

WHAT DOES THE LIVER DO?

One of the liver's most important functions is the processing of digested food. The intestines pass digested food to the liver, where some nutrients may be released into the blood and the rest stored to be used later. The liver also processes poisons in the blood and changes unwanted proteins into urea. The kidneys then remove poisons and urea from the blood and make them into urine.

WHAT IS BILE?

Bile is a yellow-green liquid made by the liver and stored in the gallbladder. From there it passes into the small intestine, where it helps to break up fatty food.

KIDNEYS

This medical thermographic image shows raised temperatures caused by activity in the body. It reveals the kidneys at work, processing the blood.

WHY DO YOU SWEAT WHEN YOU ARE HOT?

Sweating helps to cool you down. When the body becomes hot, sweat glands pump lots of salty water onto the skin. As the sweat evaporates, it takes extra heat from the body.

SWEATING

When you exercise, the body gets hot, making you sweat. Drinking replaces the lost water.

HOW MUCH DO YOU NEED TO DRINK?

You need to drink about 2½–3 pints (5 large glasses) of watery drinks a day. Most water is lost in urine and feces, but sweat and the air you breathe also contain water.

Reproduction

A baby begins when a sperm from a man joins with an egg from a woman. The cells of the fertilized egg embed in the lining of the mother's womb. Slowly the cells multiply into the embryo of a new human being.

WHERE DOES A MAN'S SPERM COME FROM?

Sperm are made in the testicles, two sacs that hang on either side of the penis in the scrotum. After puberty, the testicles make millions of sperm every day. Any sperm that are not ejaculated are absorbed back into the blood.

WHAT IS A FETUS?

A fetus is an unborn baby from eight weeks after conception until birth. In the first seven weeks, it is called an embryo. From about 24 weeks onward, babies may survive in an incubator if they are born early, but most stay in the mother's womb for the full 38 weeks.

PREGNANCY

A baby usually grows in its mother's womb for 38 weeks.

WHERE DOES THE EGG COME FROM?

When a girl is born she already has thousands of eggs stored in her two ovaries. After puberty, one of these eggs is released every month and travels down the Fallopian tube to the womb.

❯ HOW DOES AN UNBORN BABY FEED?

Most of the cluster of cells that embeds itself in the womb grows into an organ called the placenta. Food and oxygen from the mother's blood pass through the placenta into the blood of the growing baby.

HOW FAST DOES AN UNBORN BABY GROW?

NEWBORN

The average newborn weighs about 7¾ pounds. Most newborns like to sleep a lot.

You grow faster before you are born than at any other time. Three weeks after the egg is fertilized, the embryo is the size of a grain of rice. Five weeks later, almost every part of the baby has formed—the brain, eyes, heart, stomach—yet it is only the size of a thumb. By the time it is born, the baby will probably be about 20 inches long.

❯ WHAT ARE GENES?

Genes are a combination of chemicals contained in each cell. They come from your mother and father and determine all your physical characteristics, including the color of your hair, how tall you will be, and even what diseases you might get later in life.

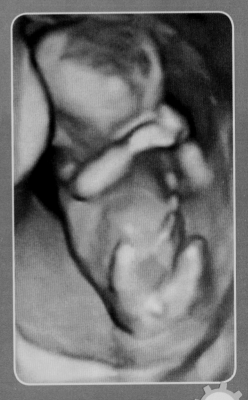

Glossary

Aboriginal
One of the original inhabitants of Australia. Aboriginals were already there when European settlers arrived.

Aquatic
Something that lives in water.

Asteroid
A piece of rock in the solar system, varying in size from a grain of dust to hundreds of miles across.

Atmosphere
A layer of gas held around a planet by gravity. The earth's atmosphere is over 500 miles thick.

Atom
Once thought to be the smallest part of a substance. We now know that atoms are made up of smaller parts known as subatomic particles.

Camouflage
Coloring that allows an animal to blend in with its background.

Carnivore
An animal that eats other animals.

Cell
The tiny unit from which all bodies are made. The smallest animals have just one cell, and the largest have many millions.

Climate
The pattern of weather in an area
All plants and animals are suited to their native climate.

Continent
One of the earth's seven large land areas, which are Africa, Antarctica, Asia, Australia, Europe, North America, and South America.

Democracy
A system of government in which leaders are chosen by people in elections. A government in which the leader is not elected is called a dictatorship.

Desert
An area of land that receives little rain. As life needs water to survive, fewer plants and animals live in deserts.

Digestion
The process of breaking down food into very small particles in the body. They can then pass into the blood to provide the body with all the substances it needs to stay healthy.

Digital
A system of storing information using a series of 0s and 1s. Machines, such as computers and cell phones, store this information electronically on microchips.

DNA
Short for deoxyribonucleic acid. DNA is arranged in a twin spiral shape, called a double helix, and contains the genetic instructions for every cell.

Echo
The repeated sound that you hear when a sound bounces back off a hard surface such as a cliff or tunnel.

Electricity
The movement of tiny particles called electrons through a substance, such as metal. This causes an electrical current that can be used as a source of power.

Electron
A subatomic particle. Along with protons and neutrons, electrons make up atoms. Electrons have a negative electrical charge and play a vital role in electricity and magnetism.

Endangered
A species, or kind, of animal that is so few in number that it is in danger of disappearing.

Equator
An imaginary line that runs round the middle of the earth.

Ethnic
A word used to describe the features held in common by a group of people. These can include language, religion, dress, or their country of origin

Evaporate
To change from a liquid into a gas, for instance when water turns into steam in a boiling saucepan.

Feces
Waste products left over from the digestive system.

Fin
A part of the body of a fish that is used for swimming.

Force
A push or a pull that makes an object speed up or slow down.

Fossil

The remains of an animal or plant that has been preserved in rock or another substance, often for millions of years.

Galaxy

A group of millions of stars held together by gravity.

Gene

The code within a cell that tells it what kind of cell it should become. In this way, our genes decide how our bodies will look.

Germs

Tiny living things, such as bacteria, that cause diseases in animals and plants.

Gravity

The force of attraction between any two objects, such as the pull between the earth and the moon.

Greenhouse effect

The warming of the earth, also known as " global warming," due to the presence of the gas carbon dioxide in the air, which stops heat escaping from the atmosphere. Pollution from burning oil and coal is causing an increase in the greenhouse effect.

Habitat

The place where an animal or plant lives.

Herbivore

An animal that eats only plants.

Hibernation

A sleep that some animals go into to survive the winter. The animal's heart rate slows down.

Ice caps

The layers of ice and snow that cover the North and South poles.

Incubation

Keeping eggs warm so that they will hatch successfully.

Insect

An animal without a backbone that has three body parts, three pairs of legs, and usually two pairs of wings.

Magma

The molten, or liquid, rock under the surface of the earth that sometimes rises up through volcanoes.

Mammal

An animal with a backbone that usually has hair on its skin. Female mammals make milk to feed their young.

Microscopic

Too small to be seen with the naked eye.

Middle Ages

A period in history that is often defined as spanning from around AD 500 to 1500.

Molecule

Tiny particle that makes up a substance. A molecule can be as small as just two atoms held together by a chemical bond.

Moon

A planet's natural satellite.

Muscle

A part of the body that is able to contract (shorten) and relax (lengthen) to produce movement.

Nerve

A bundle of fibers in the body that carries electrical signals to and from the brain.

Neutron
A subatomic particle found in the nucleus of an atom. Neutrons carry no electrical charge.

Organ
A part of an animal or plant that performs a particular task. The heart, for example, pumps blood around the body.

Photosynthesis
The process plants use to make chemicals using the sun's energy. This forms the basis for all other life as it is the only way in nature to take energy from the sun.

Plankton
The tiny plants and animals that are found floating close to the surface of ponds, lakes, and seas.

Polar
Related to the cold areas around the North and South poles.

Population
The total number of people or animals living in a particular place.

Predator
An animal that hunts and eats other animals.

Prey
An animal that is hunted by another animal for food.

Proton
A subatomic particle found in the nucleus of an atom. Protons carry a positive electrical charge.

Rain forest
Dense forest found in areas with high rainfall around the equator.

Renewable energy
A source of energy, such as wind power, which cannot be used up.

Reptile
An animal with a backbone that has four legs and a body covered by scales.

Satellite
Any object that orbits a planet, held by the planet's gravity.

Scavenger
An animal that eats dead plants or animals.

Sediment
Small pieces of rock or soil that settle at the bottom of rivers and oceans.

Senses
The ways humans and animals are able to experience the world around them. Humans have five senses: sight, hearing, touch, smell, and taste.

Skeleton
The framework of a body that holds it together. Some skeletons are inside the body, while others are outside.

Solar System
The part of space that includes the Sun, the planets that circle the Sun, and all the moons and asteroids in between.

Temperate
Areas of the world that have a mild climate and four seasons.

Tropical
Areas of the world that lie around the middle of the earth, near the equator, and are hot all year round.

Vein
Blood vessel that carries blood back to the heart. The larger veins have valves inside them to stop blood flowing the wrong way.

Vertebrate
Any animal that has a bony skeleton and a backbone. Animals without a backbone are called invertebrate.

Index

Index →

Acknowledgments

Artwork supplied through the Art Agency by Terry Pastor, Ken Oliver, Peter Ball, Myke Taylor, Stuart Jackson-Carter, Wayne Ford. Photo credits: b = bottom, t = top, r = right, l = left, m = middle.

Cover: Front cover: c Corbis, bl istockphoto.com/Pali Rao, bm istockphoto.com/Moodboard_Images, br istockphoto.com/sculpies. Front jacket flap: istockphoto.com/Floortje. Back cover: tl istockphoto.com/IngramPublishing, tm istockphoto.com/Beboy_ltd, tr istockphoto.com/Jacob Hamblin. Back jacket flap: istockphoto.com/Christopher Penler

6 Dreamstime.com/Goce Risteski, 7bl Digital Vision, 7bm NASA, 7br NASA, 8b NASA, 9b Dreamstime.com, 9t NASA, 10t NASA, 10b Joseph Sohm; ChromoSohm Inc./CORBIS, 11t Dreamstime.com/Ken Wood, 12B Dreamstime.com/Goce Risteski, 12-13r NASA, 12tm Digital Vision, 13t NASA, 13b NASA, 14t NASA, 14b NASA, 15t Dreamstime.com/Antonio Petrone, 15b NASA, 16t NASA, 16b NASA, 17t NASA, 17m NASA, 17b NASA, 18t NASA, 19m NASA, 19b NASA, 20-21b NASA, 20m NASA, 21t Dreamstime.com/Johnny Lye, 21m NASA, 22t Amos Nachoum/CORBIS, 22b NASA, 23t NASA, 23b NASA, 24t Dreamstime.com/Steven Bourelle, 24b Dreamstime.com/Daniel Gustavsson, 26b NASA, 26-27m Digital Vision, 27t iStockphoto.com, 27b Dreamstime.com, 28b Dreamstime.com/Jose Fuente, 29t Digial Vision, 29b NASA, 30-31b Dreamstime.com, 30 Digital Vision, 31t Digital Vision, 32b Dreamstime.com/Peter Hazlett, 33b Digital Vision, 34—35 Robert Everts/Getty Images, 36—37 Alessandro Bolis/Dreamstime.com, 37l Webking/Dreamstime.com, 37r Karen Moller/iStockphoto, 38—39 Jeremy Walker/Getty Images, 38 Moemrik/Dreamstime.com, 39 James Steidl/Dreamstime.com, 40—41 Philippe Bourseiller/Getty Images, 41t Denise Kappa/iStockphoto, 41b European/Getty Images, 42—43 Pavalache Stelian/Dreamstime.com, 43t Robyvannucci/Dreamstime.com, 43b Carolyne Pehora/Dreamstime.com, 44 David Pedre/iStockphoto, 45t Norbert Speicher/iStockphoto, 45b French School/Getty Images, 46—47 Robert Churchill/iStockphoto, 47l David Lentz/iStockphoto, 47r Jason Gulledge/iStockphoto, 48 DaddyBit/iStockphoto, 49t George Gower/Getty Images, 49b Erick Nguyen/Dreamstime.com, 50—51 Mike Carlson/Dreamstime.com, 51t Luciano Mortula/Dreamstime.com, 51b Rb-studio/Dreamstime.com, 52 Mansell/Time & Life Pictures/Getty Images, 53l William Wang/Dreamstime.com, 53r Matthew Scholey/Dreamstime.com, 54 Sundown/Dreamstime.com, 55t Michael Thompson/Dreamstime.com, 55b Coomerguy/Dreamstime.com, 56—57 Time Life Pictures/Mansell/Getty Images, 56 English School/Getty Images, 57 Rod Lawson/Dreamstime.com, 58t Dan Braus Photography/iStockphoto, 58b Popperfoto/Getty Images, 59 NASA, 60 Dreamstime.com/Dndavis, 61bl Dreamstime.com/Daniel Boiteau, 61bm Dreamstime.com/Elena Elisseeva, 61br Dreamstime.com, 62t Dreamstime.com/Mylightscapes, 62b Dreamstime.com/Elena Elisseeva, 63t Dreamstime.com/ Luisa Fernanda, 64b Dreamstime.com/ Pieter Janssen, 65t Dreamstime.com/Marcus Brown, 65b Dreamstime.com/Vasiliy Koval, 66t Digital Vision, 66b Kim Ludbrook/epa/Corbi, 67t Bettmann/CORBIS, 67b Royal Household handout/epa/Corbis, 68t John Deere, 68b Natalie Fobes/CORBIS, 69l Dreamstime.com/Ilya Pivovarov, 69m Digital Vision, 70t Digital Vision, 70b William Campbell/Sygma/Corbis, 71t Dreamstime.com/Dndavis, 72t Digital Vision, 72b Dreamstime.com/Kroft, 73t Dreamstime.com/Stougard, 73m NASA, 73b Dreamstime.com/Tsz01, 74t Roger Ressmeyer/CORBIS, 74b Dreamstime.com/Zinchik, 75t Dreamstime.com/Edyta Linek, 75b Ajay Verma/Reuters/Corbis, 76b Colin McPherson/Corbis, 77t Dreamstime.com/Craig Ruaux, 77b Dreamstime.com, 78t Dreamstime.com, 78b Jeremy Horner/CORBIS, 79t Dreamstime.com/Bonnie Jacobs, 79b Wendy Stone/CORBIS, 80l Dreamstime.com/David Davis, 80b Matthias Schrader/dpa/Corbis, 81t Dreamstime.com/Kiankhoon, 81b Dreamstime.com, 82t Dreamstime.com/Norman Chan, 82b Olivier Martel/Corbis, 83t Dreamstime.com, 83b Paul Barton/Corbis, 84t Dreamstime.com/Winterling, 84b Dreamstime.com/Pulsartt, 85t Dreamstime.com/Siamimages, 85b Dreamstime.com/Franz Pfuegl, 86—87 Adam Jones/Visuals Unlimited/Getty Images, 88 Peter Garbet/iStockphoto, 89t Ppmaker2007/Dreamstime.com, 89b Richard Griffin/Dreamstime.com, 90 Mikeexpert/Dreamstime.com, 91l Janehb/Dreamstime.com, 91r Tommounsey/Dreamstime.com, 92 Liang Ma/Dreamstime.com, 93t Karoline Cullen/Dreamstime.com, 93b Scheiker/Dreamstime.com, 94—95 Gumenuk Vitalij/Dreamstime.com, 95t Brenda A. Smith/Dreamstime.com, 95b Bill Kennedy/Dreamstime.com, 96 Isabel Poulin/Dreamstime.com, 97l Tessa Rath/Dreamstime.com, 97r Colleen Coombe/Dreamstime.com, 98 Larry Ye/Dreamstime.com, 99t Sandra Cunningham/Dreamstime.com, 99b Laura Bulau/Dreamstime.com, 100l Angela Vetu/Dreamstime.com, 100r Oneclearvision/iStockphoto, 101 Rene Hoffmann/Dreamstime.com, 102 Chris Hellier/Corbis, 103t Kai Zhang/Dreamstime.com, 103b Carrie Bottomley/iStockphoto, 104 Peter Elvidge/Dreamstime.com, 105t Feng Hui/Dreamstime.com, 105b Pasticcio/iStockphoto, 106—107 Marek Cech/iStockphoto, 107t Peter Pattavina/iStockphoto, 107b Mark Kolbe/iStockphoto, 108 Maxim Malevich/Dreamstime.com, 109l Ken Cole/Dreamstime.com, 109r Dean Pennala/Dreamstime.com, 110 Vova Pomortzeff/Dreamstime.com, 110—111 Lesya Castillo/Dreamstime.com, 111 Alan T. Duffy 1970/Dreamstime.com, 112—113 Ronald Wittek/Getty Images, 114—115 Ken Cole/Dreamstime.com and John Pitcher/Dreamstime.com, 114 Sters/Dreamstime.com, 115 Ryszard Laskowski/Dreamstime.com, 116 Anthony Hathaway/Dreamstime.com, 117l Valerie Crafter/iStockphoto, 117r Sandra vom Stein/iStockphoto, 118 Kitch Bain/iStockphoto, 119l Karel Broz/Dreamstime.com, 119r Anita Huszti/Dreamstime.com, 120t Yong Chen/Dreamstime.com, 120b Jean-Marc Strydom/Dreamstime.com, 121 Ian Jeffery/iStockphoto, 122—123 Neil Bradfield/iStockphoto, 122 Edward Duckitt/Dreamstime.com, 123 Jayanand Govindaraj/Dreamstime.com, 124 Chris Fourie/Dreamstime.com, 125t Romkaz/Dreamstime.com, 125b Lee Dirden/Dreamstime.com, 126 Yegor Korzh/Dreamstime.com, 127t Nicole Duplaix/National Geographic/Getty Images, 127b Gary Unwin/Dreamstime.com, 128 Martin Harvey/Corbis, 129l Ewan Chesser/Dreamstime.com, 129r Rusty Dodson/Dreamstime.com, 130 Eric Delmar/Dreamstime.com, 131t Can Balcioglu/Dreamstime.com, 131b Xavier Marchant/Dreamstime.com, 132 Eric Gevaert/Dreamstime.com, 133l Peter-John Freeman/iStockphoto, 133r George Clerk/iStockphoto, 134t Anna Yu/iStockphoto, 134b Hudakore/Dreamstime.com, 135 Sebastian Duda/iStockphoto, 136 Paul McCormick/Getty Images, 137l Joe McDaniel/iStockphoto, 137r Nico Smit/Dreamstime.com, 138—139 Tim Laman/National Geographic/Getty Images, 140 Tom Dowd/Dreamstime.com, 141t Morten Elm/iStockphoto, 141b John Pitcher/iStockphoto, 142 Jens Kuhfs/Getty Images, 143t Ken Moore/Dreamstime.com, 143b Dale Walsh/iStockphoto, 144 Evgeniya Lazareva/iStockphoto, 144—145 David Schrader/iStockphoto, 145 Paul Nicklen/National Geographic/Getty Images, 146 Romilly Lockyer/Getty Images, 146—147 Jeff Hunter/Getty Images, 147 Casey and Astrid Witte Mahaney/Lonely Planet Images/Getty Images, 148 Carol Buchanan/Dreamstime.com, 149t Jacek Chabraszewski/Dreamstime.com, 149b Sergey Kulikov/iStockphoto, 150 Mark Kostich/iStockphoto, 151t Tommounsey/Dreamstime.com, 151b iStockphoto, 152 Greg Niemi/iStockphoto, 153t Anup Shah/The Image Bank/Getty Images, 153b Mark Higgins/iStockphoto, 154 Kim Bunker/iStockphoto, 155 Jason Edwards/National Geographic/Getty Images, 156—157 Kim Bunker/iStockphoto, 157t Jerome Whittingham/Dreamstime.com, 157b Thomas Bjornstad/Dreamstime.com, 158t Janne Hämäläinen/iStockphoto, 158b Paul Edwards/Dreamstime.com, 159 Roberto A. Sanchez/iStockphoto, 160—161 iStockphoto, 161l Andrew Howe/iStockphoto, 161r Rui Saraiva/Dreamstime.com, 162 J.C. McKendry/iStockphoto, 163l Jeff Foott/Getty Images, 163r Derek Dammann/iStockphoto, 164 Dreamstime.com/Rafa Irusta, 165bl Digital Vision, 165bm Digital Vision, 165br Dreamstime.com, 166r Dreamstime.com/Marcelo Zagal, 166ml Dreamstime.com/Andreus, 167tl Dreamstime.com/Kasia75, 167b Dreamstime.com, 168t Dreamstime.com, 168b NASA, 169t Dreamstime.com/Bigmax, 170t Dreamstime.com, 170b Dreamstime.com/Daniel Gale, 171t Dreamstime.com, 172t Dreamstime.com/Holger Feroudj, 172b Dreamstime.com, 175t Dreamstiem.com/Roy Mattappallil, 176b Digital Vision, 197b Dreamstime.com, 176t Dreamstime.com/Dkye, 176b Dreamstime.com/Jason Stitt, 177t Dreamstime.com/Alan Snelling, 177b Dreamstime.com/Terdonal, 178t Dreamstime.com/Martin Green, 178b Dreamstime.com, 179tl Dreamstime.com/Nicole Waring, 179tm Dreamstime.com, 179tr Dreamstime.com/Tomasz Adamczyk, 179b Digital Vision, 180t Digital Vision, 180b Dreamstime.com/Ye Liew, 181t Dreamstime.com/Mary Lane, 181b Dreamstime.com/Elminster, 182t Dreamstime.com/Lancemichaels, 183t Dreamstime.com/Rafa Irusta, 183b Dreamstime.com, 184t Dreamstime.com/Jerry Horn, 184b Dreamstime.com/John Sartin, 185tl Dreamstime.com, 185tr Dreamstime.com/Scott Rothstein, 186tr Dreamstime.com/Attila Huszti, 186tm Dreamstime.com/Adam Borkowski, 186tl Dreamstime.com/Jose Antonio, 187tr Dreamstime.com/Visualfield, 187b Dreamstime.com, 188t Dreamstime.com/Crni_arapin, 188b Dreamstime.com, 189t Dreamstime.com, 189b Dreamstime.com/Andreas Weiss, 190—191 Peter Dazeley/Getty Images, 192 Dr. Don Fawcett/Getty Images, 193t Clouds Hill Imaging Ltd/Corbis, 193b Anette Linnea Rasmussen/Dreamstime.com, 194 3D4Medical.com/Getty Images, 195l Carolina K. Smith M.D./Dreamstime.com, 195r Peterfactors/Dreamstime.com, 196 3D4Medical.com/Getty Images, 197t Bobby Deal/Dreamstime.com, 197b Emir Memedovski/Dreamstime.com, 198 Dannyphoto80/Dreamstime.com, 199l Andres Balcazar/iStockphoto, 199r Sebastian Kaulitzski/Dreamstime.com, 200 Tihis/Dreamstime.com, 200—201 Dan McCoy/Rainbow/Getty Images, 201 Ryszard Bednarek/Dreamstime.com, 202 Kutay Tanir/iStockphoto, 203t Dannyphoto80/Dreamstime.com, 203b Rosemarie Gearhart/iStockphoto, 204l David Davis/Dreamstime.com, 204r Gordana Sermek/Dreamstime.com, 205 3D4Medical.com/Getty Images, 206 Visuals Unlimited/Corbis, 207l Tracy Hebden/iStockphoto, 207r Oguzaral/Dreamstime.com, 208—209 Kennan Harvey/Getty Images, 209l Vlad Turchenko/Dreamstime.com, 209b 3D4Medical.com/Getty Images, 210—211 Sebastian Kaulitzki/Dreamstime.com, 211l Sgame/Dreamstime.com, 211r Dannyphoto80/Dreamstime.com, 212 Sebastian Kaulitzki/Dreamstime.com, 212—213 Pete Saloutos/Corbis, 213 Stephen Coburn/Dreamstime.com, 214—215 Devan Muir/iStockphoto, 215l Jenna Duetsch/iStockphoto, 215r Koi88/Dreamstime.com, 216l Armin Rose/Dreamstime.com, 216r Bob Ainsworth/Dreamstime.com, 217 Julien Grondin/iStockphoto, 218t Anna Yu/iStockphoto, 218b Hashim Pudiyapura/Dreamstime.com.